The Teaching Assistant's Guide Effective Interaction

The Teaching Assistant's Guide to Effective Interaction is the definitive guide to teaching assistant–pupil interaction and an invaluable professional development tool for classroom support staff and the teachers who work with them. The authors' research and development work with schools has highlighted the need for specific, practical guidance on the role of the teaching assistant.

This highly practical and accessible book sets out a role for teaching assistants that focuses on developing pupils' independence and ownership of learning. Based on a classroom-tested framework and covering the main contexts in which teaching assistants work, it includes practical strategies and reflective activities to help you improve the support you provide to pupils in everyday settings. This book will help you to:

- improve your interactions with pupils
- understand the principles behind effective classroom talk
- carefully scaffold pupils' learning
- effectively work in collaboration with teachers
- support the assessment for learning process
- support group work and collaborative tasks
- deliver intervention programmes.

This book is an essential read for all teaching assistants. It will also be of interest to school leaders, SENCOs and teachers in both primary and secondary schools who wish to improve their use of teaching assistants and their own interactions with pupils.

Paula Bosanquet is Head of Subject for Education and Development at the Cass School of Education and Communities, University of East London, UK.

Julie Radford is Senior Lecturer in Special and Inclusive Education at the UCL Institute of Education, London, UK.

Rob Webster is a Researcher at the UCL Institute of Education, London, UK and co-author of *Maximising the Impact of Teaching Assistants*.

The Teaching Assistant's Guide to Effective Interaction

How to maximise your practice

Paula Bosanquet, Julie Radford and Rob Webster

Routledge
Taylor & Francis Group

LONDON AND NEW YORK

First published 2016
by Routledge
2 Park Square, Milton Park, Abingdon, Oxon OX14 4RN

and by Routledge
711 Third Avenue, New York, NY 10017

Routledge is an imprint of the Taylor & Francis Group, an informa business

British Library Cataloguing in Publication Data
A catalogue record for this book is available from the British Library

Library of Congress Cataloging in Publication Data
Bosanquet, Paula.
The teaching assistant's guide to effective interaction : how to
maximise your practice / Paula Bosanquet, Julie Radford and Rob
Webster.
pages cm
1. Teacher's assistants—Handbooks, manuals, etc. I. Radford, Julie.
II. Webster, Rob, 1976– III. Title.
LB2844.1.A8B57 2016
371.14'124—dc23
2015010395

ISBN: 978-1-138-85618-9 (hbk)
ISBN: 978-1-138-85619-6 (pbk)
ISBN: 978-1-315-71983-2 (ebk)

Typeset in Sabon
by Swales & Willis Ltd, Exeter, Devon, UK

MIX
Paper from
responsible sources
FSC
www.fsc.org   FSC® C013056

Printed and bound in Great Britain by
TJ International Ltd, Padstow, Cornwall

Contents

List of figures   vi

Introduction: teaching assistants and their roles in school   1

1 The teaching assistant as scaffolder   17

2 The value of planning the right task and pupils taking
   an active role in interactions   24

3 The principles of scaffolding   43

4 Scaffolding strategies   57

5 Assessment for learning: providing valuable feedback for
   teachers and pupils   76

6 Promoting effective group work   88

7 Delivering intervention programmes   103

   Conclusion   110

   Appendices   113
   Index   120

Figures

I.1   The Wider Pedagogical Role (WPR) model   7
2.1   The zone of proximal development   28
3.1   The scaffolding process   45
3.2   Scaffolding framework   53
5.1   The assessment for learning cycle   79
5.2   Contingent teaching cycle   84

Introduction

Teaching assistants and their roles in school

Welcome to *The Teaching Assistant's Guide to Effective Interaction: How to Maximise Your Practice*. We have written this book in response to the requests we have received from teaching assistants, the teachers who manage their work, special educational needs co-ordinators (SENCOs) and headteachers. These requests indicate that there is a lack of guidance relating to effective teaching assistant-to-pupil interaction and a clear need for a professional development tool, *especially for* classroom support staff. Our on-going work with schools has revealed the need for specific guidance that complements and extends our wider efforts to raise the profile of the teaching assistant role, and to ensure that school leaders maximise the impact of their support workforce.

Who are 'teaching assistants' and why do they matter?

We will define the terminology used in this book later, but we need to be clear from the start who we are referring to when we talk about teaching assistants. Throughout this book, we use the term 'teaching assistant' (TA for short) to refer to all school support staff who have a role directly supporting learners. Such members of staff are also known as learning support assistants (LSAs) and classroom assistants. Some senior TAs are known as higher-level teaching assistants (HLTAs). In our research, however, we have found that these titles are not applied with any consistency across schools. The main reason for this seems to be that there is no national system for differentiating between these different titles; one school's TA is another's LSA, and vice versa.

Our definition of TAs reflects the term most commonly found both nationally and internationally; although 'teacher assistant', 'teacher aide' or 'teaching aide' and 'para-educator' are more often used in the USA and Australia. Other adults who commonly work in UK classrooms include nursery nurses, nursery assistants, early years practitioners, literacy and numeracy support staff, learning mentors, foreign language assistants, and special needs and minority ethnic pupil support staff.

Our use of the term TA also reflects the definition used by the UK government to calculate the number of TAs working in schools. There has been a year-on-year rise in the number of TAs in schools since the mid-1990s. Presently, a quarter of the school workforce in mainstream schools in England is comprised of TAs. In primary and nursery schools, they make up a third (34 per cent) of the workforce, and TAs comprise 15 per cent of the secondary school workforce (Department for Education, 2015). These percentages are known as 'full-time equivalent' figures. They state that the equivalent of 255,100 members of school staff (including those in special schools) work as TAs. Yet the majority of TAs work part-time, not full-time: 91 per cent of TAs in primary and nursery schools and 69 per cent in secondary schools work part-time. So, when we talk about TAs, we are referring to many more people than would at first appear. According to the government's own headcount figures, there are more TAs working in primary and nursery schools (251,600) than teachers (242,500). In secondary schools, there are 228,800 individual teachers and 67,800 individual TAs.

We mention these figures because it is important for us to have a sense of how essential it is that schools know how to deploy TAs to maximum benefit. What TAs do in schools *really* matters because, as we shall see, their practice has a direct impact on pupil outcomes. Having so many TAs working in schools means that it is essential to ensure that everyone connected with schools – governors, headteachers, senior and middle leaders, SENCOs, teachers, pupils, parents and, of course, TAs – has a clear understanding of their role and the contribution that TAs make. This is why this book has been deliberately written to dovetail with guidance for school leaders and teachers set out in *Maximising the Impact of Teaching Assistants* by Webster, Russell and Blatchford (2016).

REFLECTION ACTIVITY

What is your job title?

Do other titles exist in your school for staff with learning support roles, other than teachers?

If so, what are the differences between these roles?

Note down the main tasks you carry out on a day-to-day basis, both inside and outside of the classroom. It may help if you think about a typical day or your most recent day.

Types of TA role

Here we describe the main roles and tasks carried out by TAs, as reflected in our research and our work with schools (more of which later). We have split the roles into two categories: pedagogical and non-pedagogical. Most TAs have a broadly pedagogical role, meaning that they support learning through direct interactions with pupils which are focused on academic tasks. Non-pedagogical roles can be thought of as 'non-teaching' roles and tasks, such as administration and roles concerning pupils' emotional and physical well-being.

We recognise that TAs work in different ways in different schools, and your role is likely to be more nuanced than those we describe below. These different roles are not always clearly differentiated. Some TAs may perform one of these roles all of the time; others may have something of a mixture and have two or more roles. In order to establish some common ground for the work ahead, we have captured key features of TAs' work at a level we think all readers will recognise. As you read about each role, you may well see tasks you will want to add to the list that you have just written.

Pedagogical TA roles

Class-based support

Most often found in primary schools, class-based TAs are assigned to a particular class, or share their time between two or more classes in a particular year group or key stage. They may be assigned to work with any of the pupils in the class, individually or in groups, and carry out a range of other activities, as directed by the class teacher. Class-based TAs often have both a pedagogical role, interacting with pupils during academic tasks set by the teacher, and a non-pedagogical role (for example, preparing resources or administering medication).

One-to-one support

Sometimes an individual pupil will have a TA allocated to support them because they have a high level of special educational need (SEN) or a disability. These pupils very often have a Statement of SEN or an Education, Health and Care Plan. One-to-one TAs need to have a general understanding of the type of SEN or disability that the pupil has, as well as an understanding of the pupil's specific needs in relation to different types of task. Often one-to-one TAs are asked to work with a group of pupils which includes the supported pupil. Research has shown that TAs who spend all or most of their time providing individual support for those with SEN frequently work with these pupils away from the classroom (Webster and Blatchford, 2013), although, as we shall discuss, this can create difficulties for the pupil.

Subject specialist or faculty-based support

These TAs are most often found in secondary schools, where they are allocated to subject departments or faculties, such as science or languages. These TAs often have a relevant qualification in the specific subject that they are supporting and, increasingly, we find that they have an undergraduate degree in the subject (e.g. physics or French language). Subject-specific TAs are similar to class-based TAs in that they provide general support in classes. They may be assigned to work with pupils across the attainment range, individually or in groups.

Intervention support

TAs may have a role in delivering intervention or booster groups. Intervention programmes tend to focus on numeracy and areas of literacy: spelling, reading, writing, phonics, speech and language, and English as an Additional Language (EAL). It is important that these TAs receive regular training in subject knowledge as well as the skills relevant to the intervention programmes they deliver, which tend to be commercially published schemes.

Leading whole classes

Leading whole classes is often undertaken by support staff with a specific role, principally HLTAs and cover supervisors. HLTAs are experienced and very capable TAs who have a higher level of responsibility than other TAs. Most schools have one or more HLTAs on their staff. It is often thought that HLTA is a qualification, but it is not; it is a status. To earn HLTA status, TAs are assessed against a set of standards, many of which are similar to the standards trainee teachers need to meet in order to obtain qualified teacher status (Blatchford, Russell and Webster, 2012). Assessment follows a needs analysis and relevant training.

Cover supervisors are employed by secondary schools to supervise lessons in the absence of a teacher. In some primary schools, TAs perform a cover supervision role in addition to their other duties. When cover supervisors were first introduced in the mid-2000s, the roles were initially carried out by TAs. One of the reasons the role was introduced was to help schools operate without the need for so many supply teachers. We have included cover supervisors in our description of TA roles because we know that many readers will be familiar with the practice of TAs leading lessons in the absence of a teacher.

Non-pedagogical support

Administrative support

Some TAs have a predominantly or entirely non-pedagogical role. These TAs might be more appropriately thought of as *teachers'* assistants, because they support teaching and learning in a non-direct way by carrying out teachers' administrative duties (e.g. photocopying and preparing resources) or tasks across the school (e.g. putting up displays or managing stock). With TAs doing these tasks, teachers are freed up to do more pedagogical tasks, such as planning and assessment. There is good evidence to suggest that having members of support staff who relieve teachers of these duties has a knock-on effect in terms of making teachers feel more positive about their workload and stress (Blatchford *et al.*, 2012). So, whilst TAs in non-pedagogical roles do not work directly with pupils, their role is essential for ensuring that teaching and learning time is maximised.

Welfare/pastoral support

A TA may have a role in supporting the emotional and social needs of pupils. A good example is the 'Emotional Literacy Support Assistant' (ELSA) scheme, which has been developed in Southampton and Hampshire (www.elsanetwork.org). The TA meets regularly with individual pupils outside the classroom and supports them in thinking through how to approach situations that they find challenging. It is important that TAs who carry out this role receive specialist training and on-going support, as they are often working with pupils who have complex emotional and/or behavioural needs. ELSAs, for example, receive regular supervision and on-going support from an educational psychologist.

Behaviour support

This role involves supporting pupils with their behaviour, rather than their learning. However, this is usually on the understanding that the former is a prerequisite for the latter. The TA works within the classroom to help pupils focus on their learning by helping them to avoid (and avoid creating) distractions and to cope with social situations they find difficult. There is often a link between the behaviour and welfare/pastoral roles of TAs.

REFLECTION ACTIVITY

Review the list you have made of the tasks that you carry out.

Which of these tasks are pedagogical?

Which of these tasks are non-pedagogical?

Which of the above categories, or mix of categories, best represents your role?

The purpose of this book

This book focuses on the pedagogical role of the TA; that is, it concerns the work of TAs who support learning directly by interacting with pupils during academic tasks, both in the classroom and in intervention sessions. We want to emphasise that, by writing a book on this topic, we are not saying that this is the most important TA role or that all TAs should be involved in pedagogy. However, it is arguably the most common TA role, and the one that most interests school leaders. 'How', they ask us, 'can we make better use of TAs who have a direct input into pupils' learning?'

To explain how we came to write this book – and why we think professional development for TAs with a pedagogical role is such an important issue – it is useful to know something about the research that we have been involved with and how it has prompted and informed the book.

Our research and consultancy work with schools has led to the development of a framework for putting into practice how TAs can interact effectively with pupils in pedagogical contexts. Put simply, this book is a professional development tool designed to give TAs the knowledge, skills and confidence to make a specific contribution to learning and for improving pupil outcomes. Our conceptualisation and development of this role stems from our particular view about the widespread use of TAs in particular teaching and learning contexts and the impact they can have on pupils, which has in turn been informed by a unique and ground-breaking research programme we have been conducting since 2003.

You may have read stories in the English media citing the findings from our research to suggest that schools should axe TA jobs.[1] Let us be clear that we do not endorse these views and, if anything, believe such an action would do huge damage to the school system. In our summary of the research below, we set the story straight. We also provide the context in terms of where this book sits within our wider campaign to improve and professionalise the role of TAs, which involves policymakers, local authorities, academy chains, teaching school alliances, schools (individually and those in clusters and partnerships) and the individuals working in them.

The impact of TAs on pupils' learning: what the research tells us

In 2009, Peter Blatchford and colleagues at the UCL Institute of Education, London, reported findings from their six-year Deployment and Impact of Support Staff (DISS) project. As its name implies, the DISS project – which is the largest study of its kind in the world – looked at how TAs were used in schools and what impact they had on the learning of 8,200 pupils in 78 primary and 92 secondary mainstream schools in England and Wales (Blatchford et al., 2012).

You can read more about the DISS project on our website (http://maximisingtas. co.uk/research.php), but to cut to the quick, the results found that the more support a pupil received from TAs, the less academic progress they made over a school year. These results were consistent across seven year groups from Years 1 to 10, and the three core subjects of English, maths and science.

You may be surprised by these results (so were the research team!), but you might sensibly argue that, as it tends to be the pupils that struggle who receive the most TA support, including those with SEN, these results are perhaps not that surprising. These pupils tend to underachieve because of other factors, so it would be reasonable to assume that this is what is reflected in the DISS project results. However, the statistical analyses the research team performed took into account the key pupil characteristics known to affect attainment and/or the allocation of TA support: SEN status, prior attainment, eligibility for free school meals[2], measures of deprivation, age, gender, and ethnicity.

So, the research team had not only found an independent effect of TA support on pupils' learning outcomes, but also that the effect was in a negative direction. There was, in other words, something connected to TAs that was strongly related to a lack of pupil progress. But what? As we explain below, it turned out that the relationship between TA support and pupil attainment had far more to do with decisions made about TAs by school leaders and teachers than with decisions made by TAs themselves. In other words, TAs were not to blame!

Explaining the DISS project results on attainment

The researchers looked in more detail at the possible explanations for the attainment findings by analysing the huge amount of data they had collected over the six years the DISS project was conducted. This included: nearly 18,000 questionnaire responses from school staff; observations of hundreds of pupils and TAs in 114 schools; 65 detailed case studies; nearly 300 interviews with school leaders, SENCOs, teachers and TAs; and transcripts of adult-to-pupil talk in 16 lessons. To find the possible causes for the surprising results, the research team identified the features of TAs' work within classrooms and pupils' experiences of being supported by TAs in learning contexts. The team hypothesised that a detailed view of what happens in everyday classroom situations would produce some clues.

The research team developed a model to explain their findings, called the Wider Pedagogical Role (WPR) model (Figure I.1).

There are five components to the model, each describing particular and important features of the TA role. Three components were of specific interest: deployment, practice and preparedness. Below, we work through the main findings from the additional DISS project analyses relating to these themes. As we do, it will become clear why we believe that media reports which appear to blame TAs for the negative impact on pupil attainment are dangerously misplaced.

Deployment

There were several key findings under this heading. The first was that most TAs spent the majority of their time in a pedagogical role, and the second was that TAs tended to be allocated to work with pupils with SEN or those falling behind their peers. Teachers, on the other hand, tended to work and interact with the whole class, rather than with groups or individuals. This might sound like old news to you, but until the DISS project was conducted, we had no systematic evidence of how TAs spent their day and how common these experiences were. One of the less understood values of research is to allow it to tell us things we *think* we already know, so we can avoid making judgments on false assumptions and test the accuracy of long-held assumptions.

The third, and perhaps most significant, conclusion concerned the effects of what is sometimes called the 'Velcro' model of TA support. Pupils with SEN were found to

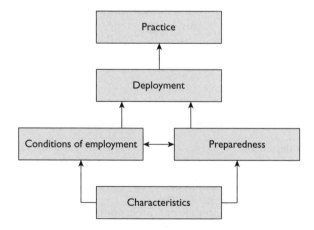

Figure I.1 The Wider Pedagogical Role (WPR) model

receive more pedagogical support from TAs than they did from teachers. The flipside to this is that these pupils became separated from the teacher, and so had fewer sustained interactions with them, compared with other (non-SEN) pupils. These pupils were 'attached' to one or more named TAs.

The effects of one-to-one TA support were particularly evident in results from another study by Rob Webster and Peter Blatchford from the DISS project team. Their Making a Statement (MAST) study (see http://maximisingtas.co.uk/research. php) focused on the day-to-day educational experiences of 48 primary school children (in Year 5) who had a Statement of SEN for learning or behavioural needs. They shadowed each pupil for a whole week, systematically logging information about their interactions on a minute-by-minute basis: where they were (inside or away from the classroom); who, if anyone, they were working with (teacher, TA or peers) and in what context (part of the class, a group, one-to-one or alone); and what they were doing (curriculum subject and task). Comparison data were also collected on 151 average-attaining pupils.

The descriptive observational results from the MAST study revealed the extent to which pupils with high-level SEN are affected by near-constant TA support (Webster and Blatchford, 2013). Across the week, it was found that pupils with Statements spent the equivalent of over a day a week with TAs outside the classroom, away from the teacher and their peers. They spent less time in whole-class teaching situations with the teacher, and had almost half as many interactions with peers as comparison pupils. Over a quarter of their interactions over the week were with a TA. In contrast, for non-SEN pupils, interaction with a TA made up a very small part of their week; one in every 50 interactions (2 per cent) was with a TA.

The DISS and MAST studies, therefore, reveal a particular unintended effect of separation that occurs when schools use TA support to meet the needs of pupils with SEN. These pupils become separated from the teaching and learning that happens in their classroom, from their teacher and their peers. Furthermore, findings from the two studies show that there has been a drift in terms of which adults have the primary responsibility for working with pupils who have SEN and, to a slightly lesser extent, with lower attainers. TAs were found to have taken on a key role in differentiating and delivering instruction to these pupils, with teachers having a reduced role. The same could not be said for the pupils that TAs worked with less often: average and higher-attaining pupils.

REFLECTION ACTIVITY

How is the role of teacher and TA different in relation to learning in your classroom?

How consistent are these roles across the school?

Practice

We use the term 'practice' to describe TAs' interactions with pupils. This is the fine-point of Deployment and the second key component of the WPR model. In terms of this book, it is the area in which we are most interested because of its central importance to learning. The DISS project was the first research study we know of to make recordings of teachers and TAs at work in the same classroom. Each adult wore a discrete recording device for the duration of a lesson which recorded their talk with pupils. The analysis of these recordings revealed three commonly occurring characteristics of TA practice that contribute to the explanation of why TA support was found to have unintended negative consequences for pupil learning.

First, TAs tended to focus on task completion, rather than learning; talk related to the end product and completing it within the given time. Second, interactions between TAs and pupils were not clearly linked to the learning aims of the task. This perhaps explains why the focus was on getting the task done. Finally, TAs tended to close down discussions rather than open them up. One example of this was the TAs' tendency to use a high proportion of closed questions, compared with teachers, who used more open questions.

REFLECTION ACTIVITY

Can you think why TAs might put more focus on getting the task done?

Do you recognise any of these tendencies in your interactions with pupils?

To avoid coming to unhelpful conclusions, it is important to put these findings into context. To do this, we need to consider how effectively TAs are prepared for the roles they undertake.

Preparedness

The third key explanatory component of the WPR model is Preparedness. Preparedness groups together the findings from the DISS project that relate to how TAs are prepared for lessons, their opportunities to meet with teachers, and their initial and on-the-job training. The research team found that teachers are often not well prepared to manage TAs and their work in classrooms; the majority reported that knowing how to work with TAs did not feature as part of their initial teacher training.

TAs were found to be underprepared in relation to supporting pupil learning on a day-to-day, lesson-to-lesson basis. A key cause of this was the lack of opportunity for detailed discussions about lesson content and the TAs' role within the lesson, the specific needs of individuals or groups of pupils, and the tasks pupils will carry out. It was found that, where teacher–TA meetings took place, it was often reliant on TAs' goodwill (e.g. working outside their paid hours).

Many TAs described how they 'went into lessons blind', not knowing any of the essential information about the lesson, and having to work 'on the hoof'. It was common for TAs to have to 'tune into' the teachers' whole-class input at the start of the lesson in order to pick up the necessary subject knowledge and information about the lesson aims and tasks. TAs were unable to prepare for the lessons effectively, so their potential contribution was frequently undermined by inadequate levels of preparation and organisation beyond their control, such as timetabling.

REFLECTION ACTIVITY

How do you obtain information about lesson content, tasks and your role in the classroom?

To what extent does this level of preparation affect your confidence going into lessons?

If you feel unconfident, what would help you feel more confident?

Characteristics of TAs and conditions of employment

To complete our summary of the findings from the DISS project, we briefly consider the two remaining components of the WPR model. The key finding under the heading of 'TA characteristics' was that TAs were found to have lower level qualifications compared to teachers. This is unlikely to come as a surprise, but it is important to bear in mind when we talk about what constitutes an appropriate role for TAs, because they are *not* teachers.

In a similar way, the key finding relating to TAs' conditions of employment substantiates another assumption often held about TAs: that they often work beyond their contracted hours. The researchers found that four out of five TAs worked extra hours on a voluntary (e.g. unpaid) basis. As we mentioned above, this is usually so that they can have valuable liaison time with teachers, because this has not been time-tabled into their school week.

Learned helplessness

Whilst it may be the biggest study of its kind, the DISS project is by no means the only research on the role and impact of TAs. Michael Giangreco (and his colleagues) at the University of Vermont in the USA is a significant researcher who has published findings on a further unintended consequence of high amounts of support: the way that pupils can become over-reliant on adults. Pupils that have somebody constantly on hand to tell them what to do next and how to do it can develop 'learned helplessness'. This describes the effect of what happens when pupils say they cannot do or understand something, or refuse to engage in a task, and TAs respond by spoon-feeding answers, giving very precise instructions, or even completing the task for the child. Pupils grow accustomed to this and the likelihood of it reoccurring increases over time. Perhaps this is not so surprising; if there was somebody sitting next to us who told us what to write next as we were writing this book (or even offered to write it for us), we might happily let them do that until it was finished!

With learned helplessness, the level of 'help' – or perhaps, more appropriately, task completion – increases as the level of pupil effort decreases. The biggest risk is that pupils become used to asking the TA 'What do I do now?', rather than thinking through for themselves how to approach a task. They may ask for help when they have a problem, because they have not received sufficient help to develop or practise independent problem-solving skills. They may also rely on the TA to tell them whether they have completed the task successfully and to what standard, rather than self-assess. This might indicate a lack of confidence in their ability or the quality of their work.

Since Velcro support is often in place from the early years, there are many pupils who have learned that if they ask their TA, or leave it long enough, the TA will do most of the task for them. Unwittingly perhaps, these pupils have, in a way, 'outsourced their learning' to the TA. It is important to tackle this because nobody wants to create a situation in which pupils cannot cope without access to high-level adult support and lack the independence and confidence to do things by themselves.

It is likely that high levels of support will be needed in the transition from one key stage to another, and from one school to another, though it will reduce dramatically (if not disappear) when pupils leave full-time education. These periods are more easily planned for than the less predictable instances of being left 'supportless' because the TA is absent or unavailable for a lesson. It is pupils' capacity to manage these day-to-day, lesson-by-lesson situations to which we need to attend.

Without the skills needed to plan tasks, problem-solve and evaluate what they have done, children and young people – regardless of whether they have SEN – will not be able to operate independently and achieve. Two particular scenarios should give us pause for reflection. First, whether we like it or not, there is a fairly relentless focus in the UK education system of preparing (some might say drilling) pupils for end-of-school examinations, such as SATs and GCSEs. Some pupils receive additional support in exams from TAs, although the rules state that TAs are limited to reading questions and scribing responses. So, at the exact moment we need pupils to be self-sufficient and confident in the exam hall, we pull away the type of support that has characterised their educational life to date.

The second scenario concerns the long-term implications for life beyond education. At least once a year – usually around the time that exam results are published – there are reports in the media from business leaders and captains of industry, bewailing the fact the high numbers of young people entering the world of work are seemingly unable to organise themselves, use their initiative, or address and persist with challenges. When we started writing this book in the summer of 2014, the Confederation of British Industry released results from a survey 'spelling out exactly where the business community's concerns and priorities lie in the UK's education system'. Over half of British firms, the CBI reported, were 'concerned about the resilience and self-management skills of school leavers and a third with their attitude towards work'.[3]

There are many disputes within education, but if there is one thing that draws almost unanimous approval, it is the idea that all children should be equipped with the skills to manage themselves and their learning as independently as possible. And as they get better at doing this, so their capacity for coping with life's bigger, scarier and less predictable challenges will improve.

REFLECTION ACTIVITY

Do you recognise signs of learned helplessness in any of the pupils that you work with?

Are there any aspects of your practice that might feed learned helplessness?

An alternative model for using TAs: the Maximising the Impact of TAs (MITA) approach

The research evidence on TA impact in everyday classrooms can be, and has been, used to mount a case for vastly reducing the number of TAs in schools. To be clear, although we understand how this view has come about, we do not share or endorse it. There is a much wider context within which TAs operate which has a bearing on how effective they can be when working with pupils. This involves teachers and wider school structures. Three components of the WPR model – deployment, preparedness and conditions of employment – need to be addressed at a school level in order to ensure that a fourth component – TA practice – is as effective as it can be.

Improving deployment, preparedness and TAs' conditions of employment is the focus of our sister book, *Maximising the Impact of Teaching Assistants: Guidance for School Leaders and Teachers* (Webster *et al.*, 2016) and our wider campaign (which we call MITA) to improve and professionalise the role of TAs, and ensure schools use TAs in ways that maximise outcomes for all pupils. The key elements of MITA are:

- Schools need a clearly thought through strategy about how and when teachers and TAs are deployed to work with individuals and groups of pupils.
- Teachers have a good understanding of the development and needs of the pupils in the class.
- Teachers take on responsibility for planning and working with groups and individuals, and that this includes working with those pupils who have SEN and those falling behind.
- Teachers are well prepared for their role as manager of other adults that work with pupils in their class. Managing the work of TAs is a skill that needs to be learned alongside other aspects of the teaching role.[4] This involves having an understanding of the pedagogical role of the TA (as described in this book) and the confidence and ability to manage and work with TAs, and to use their skills to add value to what teachers do.
- TAs and teachers have allocated time to discuss planning and the progress of pupils.
- TAs are provided with information about lesson content, their role in the lesson, which pupils they will work with and the expected outcomes. There should also be a mechanism for TAs to feed back information (specified by the teacher) at the end of the lesson.
- TAs are provided with regular training relevant to their role.
- TAs are regularly observed and given constructive feedback, and are included in the annual performance management cycle.

REFLECTION ACTIVITY

Where would you say your school is in relation to each of the points above?

It is important to make clear – as we do to school leaders that participate in the MITA programme or attend MITA events[5] – that the process of rethinking and improving the ways TAs are used is *not* a substitute for addressing the overall provision made for disadvantaged pupils, lower attainers and those with SEN. It is essential that schools thoroughly review and address the needs of all pupils, first and foremost, through high quality teaching. Only then can school leaders deal with the questions about TA deployment across the school and how to organise classrooms effectively so that TAs add value to what teachers do. As these are decisions that are outside of TAs' control, this should leave us in no doubt that, in the widest sense, improving outcomes for pupils and making the best use of TAs are school leadership issues.

MITA, then, not only addresses the problems identified through the research relating to how schools (mis)use TAs, but aims to put in place a stronger, positive alternative. We recognise that there is limited use in advising teachers and TAs to avoid particular unproductive practices; they need guidance on effective alternatives to use instead. This book is a major and critical component of the MITA process. Our motivation for writing it is to put forward an alternative view for TAs' pedagogical practice in detail, and in such a way that TAs are empowered to take their work and their contribution to learning into their own hands, and to do so in ways that school leaders and teachers would endorse and support.

Who is this book for?

The primary audience for this book is, of course, TAs working in a range of educational settings: early years, primary and secondary schools, special schools and alternative provisions. This book has been designed to contribute to their professional development in 'effective scaffolding', in both a formal and informal sense. It can be used as the basis for school-based in-service training, to support formal courses for TAs (including foundation degrees) and individual study.

This book will be of interest to teachers too, as they have the responsibility for organising the work of TAs on a day-to-day basis. Therefore, it is important that teachers are aware of the skills their TAs have, so that they can deploy them in the most effective ways. Furthermore, if teachers and TAs have the same knowledge relating to the principles and practices of scaffolding, it is likely to strengthen their partnership in the classroom.

Finally, we expect SENCOs and headteachers to read this book, as it was their requests for practical guidance for TAs that prompted us to write it! School leaders are under increasing pressure to ensure that their strategic decision-making enables TAs to make a meaningful contribution to teaching and learning, and there is a clear need for guidance and resources to support them in this area of school improvement. The guidance in this book and *Maximising the Impact of TAs* gives school leaders an evidence-based package for achieving this.

Chapter summary

Each chapter in this book has been designed to unpack and explore a specific aspect of the pedagogical role of the TA. Below is a brief summary of the key chapters. A final chapter summarising the impact of the work described concludes this book.

Chapter 1: The teaching assistant as scaffolder

First, we introduce our framework for scaffolding learning that structures the book.

Chapter 2: The value of planning the right task and pupils taking an active role in interactions

This chapter discusses the key theories which are the foundations for the framework for scaffolding learning. These theories are social constructivism, scaffolding, dialogic teaching and mindsets.

Chapter 3: The principles of scaffolding

Here we discuss the theory of scaffolding in more detail and how TAs need to interact with pupils during a task in order to maximise their learning experience.

Chapter 4: Scaffolding strategies

This chapter provides more detail on each level of our scaffolding framework in turn, giving examples of specific interactive strategies that TAs can use to develop pupils' independent learning. We use transcripts and case studies to demonstrate how these have worked in real-world situations.

Chapter 5: Assessment for learning: providing valuable feedback for teachers and pupils

In this chapter, we consider how TAs can support the teacher's job of assessment. We look at how teachers and TAs can work together to ensure that the teacher can accurately assess the development of each pupil and plan for their future learning needs.

Chapter 6: Promoting effective group work

This chapter discusses the importance of pupils being able to work with one another on collaborative activities and draw on each other as sources of support. It provides strategies TAs can use to facilitate group work effectively.

Chapter 7: Delivering intervention programmes

Many TAs deliver intervention or 'catch-up' programmes. This chapter discusses the key things to think about when TAs deliver such programmes, including: working with scripted materials; subject knowledge; accurate assessment; and how to link learning in intervention sessions with learning in the classroom.

As a TA, you may not be involved in every aspect of work that we cover in this book, so some chapters may be more relevant to you than others. All TAs will find it helpful to work through Chapters 2, 3 and 4 in order, as each of these chapters build on the content of the one before.

Throughout the book, you will find practical activities and opportunities to pause and reflect on particular questions or issues, to complete a task, or to plan something to try in your own practice. Where relevant, spaces have been provided for you to record your responses and to keep a record of your professional development. You can, of course, work through this book by yourself, but you may wish to share this experience with colleagues. We see particularly powerful possibilities for schools that make time and space for TAs to work together with a senior leader on these activities, as this can provide valuable opportunities for planning changes at the school level.

A note on names and language

Where we have used examples from our research in classrooms, we have referred to the individuals involved by their gender, but not their name. Names used are not pupils' real names.

Throughout this book, we have sought to avoid using language that might unintentionally reinforce gender stereotypes. However, on occasions, doing so can render important sentences a little cumbersome to read. Where this is the case, we hope we will be forgiven for referring to pupils and/or adults by gender (e.g. by using he/she; him/her). To ensure balance, we have alternated our use of gendered language between chapters.

Notes

1 See: www. dailymail.co.uk/news/article-2334853/Army-teaching-assistants-faces-axe-Education-department-attempts-save-4billion-cost-year.html (accessed 4 September 2014); www.thesunday times.co.uk/sto/news/uk_news/Education/article1268217.ece (accessed 4 September 2014).
2 Prior to the introduction of universal free school meals in 2014 for all children in Reception and Key Stage 1.
3 www.cbi.org.uk/media-centre/the-point/2014/07/jcs-education-blog/ (accessed 4 September 2014).
4 The DISS project recommended that all teachers should receive training in managing the work of TAs as part of their initial teacher training, and this should also feature strongly in on-going professional development.
5 For more on the MITA programme and training, visit www.maximisingtas.co.uk/

References

Blatchford, P., Russell, A. and Webster, R. (2012) *Reassessing the impact of teaching assistants: How research challenges practice and policy.* Oxon: Routledge.
Department for Education (2015) *School workforce in England: November 2014.* Available online at: www.gov.uk/government/statistics/school-workforce-in-england-november-2014(accessed 11 July 2015).
Webster, R. and Blatchford, P. (2013) The educational experiences of pupils with a Statement for special educational needs in mainstream primary schools: Results from a systematic observation study. *European Journal of Special Needs Education*, 28(4), pp. 463–479.
Webster, R., Russell, A. and Blatchford, P. (2016) *Maximising the impact of teaching assistants: Guidance for school leaders and teachers*, second edition. Oxon: Routledge.

Further reading

Giangreco, M. F. (2010) One-to-one paraprofessionals for students with disabilities in inclusive classrooms: Is conventional wisdom wrong? *Intellectual and Developmental Disabilities*, 48, pp. 1–13. Available online at: www.uvm.edu/~cdci/archives/mgiangre/IDD2010%20 48(1)%201-13.pdf (accessed 16 April 2015).

Radford, J., Blatchford, P. and Webster, R. (2011) Opening up and closing down: how teachers and TAs manage turn-taking, topic and repair in mathematics lessons. *Learning and Instruction*, 21, pp. 625–635.

Webster, R. and Blatchford, P. (2012) Supporting learning?: How effective are teaching assistants?, in P. Adey and J. Dillon. (Eds) *Bad education: Debunking educational myths.* Maidenhead: OUP. Available online at: http://maximisingtas.co.uk/research/the-edta-project. php/

Webster, R. and Blatchford, P. (2013) Worlds apart? How pupils with statements lead a life away from the class. Findings from the Making a Statement project. *Assessment and Development Matters*, 5(1), Leicester: British Psychological Society. Available online at: http://maximisingtas.co.uk/research/the-mast-study.php/

Chapter 1

The teaching assistant as scaffolder

Introduction

In this first chapter, we would like you to complete a short self-evaluation on your current understanding of some of the key concepts covered in this book. We then give some context on the TA role and outline the particular teaching and learning role for TAs we have developed through our research, our work with schools and the training programmes we run. This makes clear what we think the roles and responsibilities of the TA and the teacher should be in relation to the pupils in their class – a point often overlooked both in theory and in practice. Finally, we introduce the scaffolding framework that structures the material in the rest of this book.

Self-evaluation

Before we continue, we would like you to audit your current level of understanding and skills in the areas that we cover in this book. This will help you to identify which parts of the book will be particularly helpful to you. It will also help you to track and record your learning and understanding of key concepts and issues. This will be useful not only as you work your way through the book, but when you reflect on your practice as part of your wider and on-going professional development.

In the table below, we have listed the learning outcomes this book is designed to meet. Use the key below to give yourself a score from 1 to 5 to describe your current understanding in each area and enter it in the 'before' column. This score is intended for your own use only, although you might choose to share it with your mentor or line manager when discussing the training and support that you need. It does not matter if your initial score is low.

Key to scoring:

1 – I do not understand this

2 – I am not very sure about this

3 – I have a fair idea of this

4 – I have a good understanding of this

5 – I fully understand this.

Area of understanding	Before score (1–5)	After score (1–5)
Understanding the complementary roles and responsibilities of the teacher and TA in the classroom		
Understanding scaffolding as a theory		
Understanding what 'pupil independence' means in relation to scaffolding		
Understanding what kind of talk best supports learning		
Understanding prompting, clueing and modelling as scaffolding strategies		
Understanding when and how to use the above strategies		
Understanding the features of effective group work for pupils		
Understanding the key issues which need to be conisdered when delivering intervention sessions		
Understanding assessment for learning		
Planning ways of putting the above strategies into practice		
Total score		

Your continuing professional development

After you have read this book and had the opportunity to put some of the ideas into practice, revisit the table and score yourself again in the 'after' column. The intention is that you will score higher than your initial score as a result of engaging with this book. Or it might be that your perception of certain areas on which you feel secure are challenged and your understanding is reshaped by what we have to say. The self-evaluation table is a simple way of recording your assessment of your learning.

Once you have completed both columns, use the CPD form in Appendix 1 to identify and plan a way forward for your on-going development. Using the form, you can first locate the general area in which you want to improve, which you can split into specific targets. This follows a process we will talk much about in this book, called setting process success criteria. You can enlist the support of other TAs and teachers in identifying areas for improvement and how your needs might be met (e.g. via training or in-school mentoring). You will find a worked example of the CPD form in Appendix 2 to help you.

Introducing the pedagogical teaching assistant role

This book is about TAs in pedagogical roles. We conceptualise the pedagogical role of the TA in a very specific way, which we outline here. Before we do, it is important to recognise and accept that the TA role is not the same as that of a teacher. This might be an obvious statement, but both the DISS and MAST projects found that schools can and do use TAs, and place demands on them, as if they were teachers. A key aim of the MITA approach described in the previous chapter is to encourage school leaders to ensure that the roles and responsibilities of teachers and TAs are clarified, clear, consistently applied and understood by all staff. Expectations and demands placed on TAs, especially in relation to learning outcomes, must also be properly calibrated.

This distinction between roles is important and recognised in the SEN Code of Practice (DfE/DoH, 2015). The Code makes it clear that the teacher is 'responsible and accountable for the progress and development of the pupils in their class, including where pupils access support from teaching assistants or specialist staff' (p. 99). It is the teacher's responsibility to know the levels of development of all of their pupils, to assess their progress and to ensure that the curriculum is accessible to pupils with SEN and disabilities by appropriately differentiating tasks and putting in place an alternative where pupils' needs demand (for example, a booster intervention programme). This work should be done with support from the special educational needs coordinator (SENCO) who is the school's senior lead on matters relating to SEN and inclusion.

We can use the stipulations set out in the Code of Practice relating to teachers' responsibilities to help us define the space in which we can identify a clear and consistent role for TAs. We argue that the TA role should be complementary to that of the teacher, with each being very clear about where their own and each other's responsibilities lie. In this way, the TA role must be seen as making a distinct contribution to teaching and learning. This is why, throughout this book, we discuss the role of the teacher as well as the TA, in order to clarify what we consider to be the most effective role for each during episodes of teaching and learning.

As a result of the way that the TA role has developed in schools over the years, it is not unusual to find TAs who have taken on significant responsibility for the planning and assessment of pupils with SEN. However, we are clear that the TA role should not include planning for groups or individuals. It is the teacher's responsibility to ensure that the curriculum is accessible to all pupils through appropriately differentiated tasks. However, we think that TAs should be encouraged to contribute to the assessment for learning cycle through recording information about how pupils work towards specific task outcomes, and offering their thoughts and observations (see Chapter 5). To be clear, TAs should not have overall responsibility for the assessment of, or planning for, the pupils they work with.

So what should the role of the TA be? Since TAs work with small groups and individuals, they are in the unique position of being able to constantly monitor the step-by-step progress pupils make towards achieving learning goals. From this vantage point, TAs can provide immediate feedback and give targeted support with parts of the task that pupils find difficult. This is called *scaffolding* and it is the key to ensuring that pupils become able to work more independently. Effective scaffolding ensures that pupils are fully engaged in the task, and that potential learning is maximised. It also ensures that, over time, pupils develop the capability to carry out tasks without support and have the confidence in themselves to attempt more challenging tasks.

In our most recent studies, we have set out a very clear role for the TA as the scaffolder of pupils' learning (Radford, Bosanquet, Webster, Blatchford and Rubie-Davies, 2014; Radford, Bosanquet, Blatchford and Webster, 2015). We have found that, given a good understanding of scaffolding and its importance, TAs can be highly effective in many distinctive ways. Most of the children that TAs work with have a range of needs related to language, learning, self-esteem and the confidence to partici-pate in the busy life of the classroom. As a result, they may not readily contribute to class or group discussions and often find it difficult to answer the teacher's questions. Our work has shown that, because TAs know the children very well (and sit near them), they are in a prime position to support them emotionally, keep them moti-vated, boost their self-esteem and keep them on-task. This is what we call the *support* role of the TA and it is crucial for getting children ready to learn. When children make mistakes (which inevitably is common, regardless of their learning needs), TAs can provide the reassurance that this is a healthy part of learning and encourage them to think for themselves to work out what to do next. This is what we call the *repair* role of the TA. Finally, we have outlined a third scaffolding responsibility (called the *heuristic* role) that is associated with helping children to think about learning strate-gies. This is essential if the TA's aim is to help children to become more autonomous and independent.

Teachers do not have the same opportunities as TAs to scaffold for all of the pupils in the class, as it is not possible to closely monitor and engage with large numbers of learners in the way that TAs do. So we argue that the TA has a clear role in providing scaffolded support during tasks and providing the teacher with accurate feedback on the extent and type of support needed for pupils to be able to complete tasks success-fully. For teachers, this type of feedback is essential for ensuring that tasks for the next lesson are appropriately targeted and build on what pupils have learned and achieved.

The role we set out for TAs in this book seeks to capitalise on the greater avail-ability for 'quality talk time' TAs have with pupils, compared with teachers. In our conceptualisation, the TA's role is defined by the interactions they ought to have with learners. The specific types of interaction we cover are distinct, but complementary, to the types of interactions teachers have with pupils. We argue the guidance set out in this book could potentially transform TAs' practice.

Transforming the role, purpose and contribution of TAs

We believe that it is high-time for a nationally joined-up picture in relation to the various roles and responsibilities of TAs, which is needed to provide a clear basis for job descriptions for both TAs and teachers. Schools need to address the wider issues of organisational change, and more needs to be done by local authorities, academy chains and school clusters, alliances and partnerships to provide professional devel-opment opportunities and to facilitate the sharing of good practice. There should also be an entitlement to on-going high-quality training for TAs, which is targeted to the needs of individuals and the specifics of their role. For TAs with a pedagogical role, this means opportunities to learn and practise specific scaffolding strategies.

We are of the view that improving the way TAs interact with pupils will help to create for them a new professional identity. The basis for this identity will come from evidence that their specific contribution to learning can be directly associated with improved pupil outcomes. A clear role and purpose underpinning TAs' contributions will also raise their status and value in schools.

The aim of this book is to give TAs the tools to begin to improve their own practice as part of this vision. However, as we indicated earlier, action is required at all levels of the education system to fully transform the role, purpose and contribution of TAs. This is the focus of *Maximising the Impact of Teaching Assistants* (Webster, Russell and Blatchford, 2016), which is designed to maximise the overall effectiveness and sustainability of the practices we discuss in this book, by improving the ways in which school leaders and teachers use TAs.

Of course, change on this scale will take time, but this does not mean TAs have to wait until these conditions are met to receive training. We want TAs to do what professionals do, and take control of developing their own practice. Improving the interactions you have with pupils on a moment-by-moment basis is something of which you can take ownership and that will make a noticeable difference to the learning of pupils you work with.

A framework for scaffolding learning

So, as a TA, how do you improve the interactions you have with pupils through scaffolding? We will discuss scaffolding in detail in Chapter 3, but here we provide a brief overview. Scaffolding is a quite ubiquitous phrase in schools, but the practice it is used to describe is often some distance from the very specific set of skills we have in mind. For us, scaffolding involves:

- recognising a task as a series of smaller learning goals;
- carefully observing the progress of the pupils as they complete each part of a task;
- only intervening if the pupil has not been able to overcome a difficulty independently (giving them time to try by themselves first);
- giving specific help or feedback when a pupil needs help with a part of a task;
- providing the minimal amount of help needed to achieve.

Throughout the scaffolding process, the focus should be on encouraging the pupil to think of strategies they can use to solve the problem for themselves. To put it into a sentence, your role is to help pupils to know what to do when they do not know what to do. This is more difficult than it sounds!

It is easy to be drawn into providing more help than is needed, particularly if you feel under pressure for pupils to complete the work or if you are concerned that the pupil is held back by, or is becoming upset with, being unable to do part of the task. Sometimes TAs 'over support' (e.g. providing more help than is really needed) as a strategy to contain the behaviour of a pupil who is frustrated at being unable to access the learning, because their reactions may affect others in the class.

However, scaffolding is the key to providing a quality learning experience. When carried out correctly, scaffolding leads to:

- *Greater independence*: pupils are able to plan the next steps, problem-solve and review what they have done. They are able to do these things because the TA has helped them to develop these skills over time.
- *The ability to cope with learning challenges and setbacks*: often referred to as 'resilience', pupils are more able to persist with a learning challenge by drawing on a range of problem-solving strategies. The safety net of support remains accessible when these strategies fail.
- *Developing a relationship with failure*: TAs often support vulnerable pupils who have an ingrained fear of failure. They are reluctant to attempt something for fear of getting it wrong, so reinforcing a perception of themselves as a poor learner. The skills of scaffolding can help pupils accept mistakes and failures as an inevitable part of learning and, indeed, as an opportunity to learn.
- *A deeper engagement in, and appreciation of, learning for learning's sake*: pupils view challenges as a way of improving their learning skills. Ultimately, there is much to gain from TAs helping to instil within pupils a reassuring sense that what is important is the learning process, rather than just getting the answer right or completing the task. Indeed, improved outcomes and grades are more likely when pupils have a grip on their learning processes and a language to describe it.
- *Accessing the teacher for support when needed*: pupils are confident about asking subject specialists (teachers) for help when they do not understand a concept or how to do a task. This is particularly important in secondary schools when TAs may not have the level of subject knowledge needed to answer technical questions. From the beginning of their school career, all pupils need to feel confident in asking the teacher for help, with TAs providing vital support in terms of helping pupils identify the particular problem (i.e. which bit they are stuck with) and to formulate specific questions.
- *Greater opportunities for peer interaction*: pupils can also develop confidence to ask their peers questions about learning, as well as teachers. Being able to talk to their classmates about learning and to compare and verify understandings are important skills to develop. TAs have a role in facilitating these exchanges.
- *Less risk of stigmatisation*: some pupils, especially in secondary schools, can feel stigmatised by having 'a constant adult helper', as it makes them look to others as 'unable' and 'different'. When pupils have the skills and opportunities to work independently, accessing teacher and peer support in the same way as other pupils when they require it, their self-confidence grows. Also, as a result, TAs become invaluable as they can spread their support across the classroom, benefiting a greater number of pupils.

All of the above can be achieved by having a consistent approach to how TAs interact with pupils. However, moving pupils to a point where they are able to work more independently will not be achieved overnight. We have found that the time it takes to see changes is contingent on how dependent the pupil has become on adult support: the more dependent the pupil has become, the more resistant they are likely to be to having to solve problems by themselves (this is hard work after all!) and learn the skills of self-scaffolding. However, small changes are usually seen quickly and, once the pupil knows that the TA is going to be consistent in expecting them to work more independently, progress becomes self-sustaining. For some pupils, the journey to self-reliance is unlikely to be smooth; there will be backtracking and stalling along the way. But this is entirely consistent with the messiness and unpredictably of learning; it rarely occurs in a straight line. Once pupils start to achieve as a result of their independent efforts, their self-esteem and confidence improves and they become keener to try things by themselves. We now know of classes where pupils challenge themselves to see how much they can do without support.

If this is beginning to sound like you are doing yourself out of a job, think again! Our view is that TAs' support should be for *all* pupils in the class and not restricted to those with SEN. The guidance in *Maximising the Impact of Teaching Assistants* (Webster *et al.*, 2016) makes it clear that schools should use TAs in ways that free teachers up to provide high-quality teaching to those who need it most, when they need it most. So when the teacher is with a particular individual or group, addressing technical learning problems, your skills will be required by other pupils in the class when they hit a problem in their learning.

Summary

In this chapter, we have clarified how we see the role of the TA, focusing on their key responsibility for supporting pupils to become more independent. We have outlined why this is important and also the issues which school leaders need to attend to in order to maximise the effectiveness of their TA workforce. In the following chapter, we begin to consider the theories and research that provide the grounding for this book.

References

Department for Education and Department of Health (2015) *Special educational needs and disability code of practice: 0 to 25 years. Statutory guidance for organisations which work with and support children and young people who have special educational needs or disabilities.* Available online at: www.gov.uk/government/uploads/system/uploads/attachment_data/file/398815/SEND_Code_of_Practice_January_2015.pdf (accessed 20 February 2015).

Radford, J., Bosanquet, P., Webster, R., Blatchford, P. and Rubie-Davies, C. (2014) Fostering learner independence through heuristic scaffolding: A valuable role for teaching assistants. *International Journal of Educational Research*, 63, pp. 116–126.

Radford, J., Bosanquet, P., Blatchford, P. and Webster, R. (2015) Scaffolding learning for independence: Clarifying teacher and teaching assistant roles for children with special educational needs. *Learning and Instruction*, 36, pp. 1–10.

Webster, R., Russell, A. and Blatchford, P. (2016) *Maximising the impact of teaching assistants: Guidance for school leaders and teachers*, second edition. Oxon: Routledge.

Chapter 2

The value of planning the right task and pupils taking an active role in interactions

Introduction

In this chapter, we discuss the theory and research underpinning the scaffolding framework we introduced in Chapter 1. Compared to the chapters that follow, this chapter is somewhat less practical. You might be tempted to skip this part of the book, but please don't! Understanding why and how we have developed the framework is important for being able to use it effectively.

We start by introducing a key theory of how we think and learn, called 'social constructivist learning theory'. What this means is actually nowhere near as complicated as the name might suggest. What we understand about the process of learning something new is key to the decisions we make about how best to support pupils' learning. Understanding some key concepts of learning theory will help you to make the most of this book. We then consider the idea of dialogic talk and how social constructivist learning theory can be used effectively in the kind of everyday teaching and learning situations in which, as a TA, you find yourself. How pupils view their own abilities and achievements completes our theory jigsaw. So finally, we explain the significance of 'fixed and growth mindsets', and how these dispositions can affect pupils' engagement and learning.

How do we learn?

REFLECTION ACTIVITY

What ideas do you have about how people learn? Make a note of these and add to or modify them as you read each section of this chapter.

Arguments about how pupils learn are as old as formal education itself. The curriculum, assessment and processes of planning and teaching are all underpinned by a theory of how we, as a society, think pupils learn best. Theories have influenced policy and practice, with ideas falling in and out of favour as new evidence emerges. Of all the ideas about how learning takes place, the one we think is best for explaining and developing TA-to-pupil talk is *social constructivism*. This theory was developed in the 1930s by a Russian psychologist called Lev Vygotsky. It is only since his work was translated into English, and then adapted for a different education system in the 1980s, that his ideas have become known more widely. Vygotsky's ideas have grown and developed over time as more people have applied them to different teaching and learning contexts.

Vygotsky's work was itself a response to earlier work by a Swiss psychologist called Jean Piaget, who developed *constructivist* learning theory. It is important to understand constructivism as it helps us to understand why Vygotsky added the word 'social'.

Constructivist learning theory

Constructivist learning theory argues that we construct our own ideas individually. We interact with the world around us from birth, by making links between known and new ideas. The mental structures linking ideas together are called 'schema'. A schema might be very small or very large. A small schema links the word 'chair' with the concept of 'sitting'. A larger, more abstract, schema links a set of interlocking ideas to give us constructs such as 'morality' or 'mathematics'. These schema, Piaget (1977) said, grow larger as we add new ideas gained from experience. We add new ideas to our schema through a process called 'assimilation'. Some new ideas or linkages are harder to assimilate than others. They might not make sense at first, or they might be difficult to hold alongside our existing preconceptions. For example, our notion of chocolate being delicious conflicts with what we know it can do to our teeth and waistline! Reorganising our schema, so that this new information fits and the connections make sense, is called 'accommodation'.

You may have seen concept maps (or mind maps) used in classrooms. A concept map starts with a single word, which is often a broad concept such as 'food'. Other associated words and ideas (e.g. vegetables, meat, fruit and chocolate) are linked to this using lines or arrows. Relationships between words can also be made: fruit and vegetables are 'healthy' food; chocolate is 'unhealthy'. This process can help a pupil to map out what they already know about a topic, giving both them and us an idea of their schema it that area. We revisit the idea of concept maps in Chapter 5, as they can be very helpful in the assessment for learning cycle.

'Cognition' describes all the mental processes we need in order to learn and understand things. We develop new and more complex ways of thinking about things as we age, so cognitive development needs to be considered, just as physical development does. Piaget viewed cognitive development as a process that mainly happened inside the mind of the individual. Although he discussed how interactions with others could prompt a child to adjust their schema, he argued that if left alone to interact with the world around them, all children would show cognitive development.

REFLECTION ACTIVITY

What do you think about Piaget's view that learning happens 'in isolation'?

Social constructivist learning theory

Vygotsky, however, believed interactions had a far greater role in cognitive development. The learning theory developed from his work is known as *social* constructivism because he saw interactions with other people as the key to learning. As you will be aware, classroom talk between adults and pupils is indeed essential to learning. This is why this particular theory is as essential to understanding the talk of TAs as it is to the talk of teachers.

Rather than cognitive development happening in isolation in the mind of the individual, Vygotsky argued that development mainly happens as a result of interacting with other people. Interaction with others helps us to decide what is important in our society – that is, what we need to learn – right from birth. The Vygotskian view of learning echoes an idea from Mikhail Bakhtin (1984), another Russian scholar, who argued that knowledge should not be seen as being transmitted (for example, from adult to child) as ready-made and fully-formed. Knowledge is built, or co-constructed, through a genuine two-way dialogue. In other words, knowledge and skills are not simply passed from one generation to the next, as if it were an easy-to-swallow pill. To understand what it is important to know and to be able to do in society has to be 'agreed to' by us. We must negotiate what is relevant, what is important for us to achieve and how to best achieve it.

This means that, over time, the knowledge and skills considered important in society will change because the goals people consider to be important and relevant will change. A good example of this can be seen in the on-going development of new technology. Those of us who did not have access to smartphones and tablet computers while growing up will have had to actively seek out ways of learning how to use these items. Often our knowledge and skill is acquired through interacting with someone who has expertise in the area. There will be some of us who still prefer to use 'non-technological' solutions to achieve our goals because we are not yet convinced that using technology is a more effective and efficient way to do something – for example, writing and posting a letter rather than sending an email.

Nowadays, children have access to smartphones and tablets from a very young age. And some, it seems, become adept at using them at a quicker pace than their parents. It is because they have interacted with us as *we* use them, and interacted with other children (either physically or virtually), that they know how to use the technology to achieve goals. They see these technologies as important because of the goals they help adults achieve; for example, helping us to communicate with other people and providing us with entertainment. However, we do not sit young children down and give them a formal lesson in 'how to use a tablet computer'. Instead, this learning is acquired through on-going interaction, modelling, asking and answering questions and allowing them the opportunity to explore the technology for themselves. As these children grow up, the tools they use will change and be replaced by better technology. Some of the knowledge and skills they have learned will be taken up by their own children – but not all of it. Only what remains relevant is likely to stick. Also, this information may be applied in different ways, as what can be achieved with technology also changes and grows with time.

So, social constructivists believe that everything we learn is first encountered and acquired through interaction with others, and that this learning is then internalised (or stored) in our minds. We are motivated to achieve things we see as important. We decide what these things are as a result of interacting with those around us. We learn how to reach goals by performing actions using language and other tools (like gesture and manipulating physical objects) and through interacting with others who have greater knowledge and understanding of how to achieve these goals. It is argued that the only reason we developed language was as a way to get things done *within a specific culture* (Bruner, 1983). In other words, there is a reason behind everything we do.

The zone of proximal development

Vygotsky's ideas about the crucial role of social interaction in learning and Piaget's ideas about cognitive development (which suggests a minimal role for interaction) do not necessarily conflict. Broadly speaking, children go through phases of development which have a natural limit to what they can achieve at any given point. For example, no matter how hard you tried, you could not teach a new born baby to read! However, rather than waiting for a child to reach a developmental point 'in their own time', they can be supported to move through these phases more quickly and easily through interaction. This is achieved by the adult working with the child on tasks that are within their 'zone of proximal development' (ZPD). Vygotsky described the child's ZPD as: 'the distance between the actual developmental level, as determined by individual problem solving, and the level of potential development, as determined through problem solving under adult guidance or with more capable peers' (Vygotsky, 1978, p. 86). We can simplify that somewhat by saying that the ZPD is the area where the child's limit of what they know and are able to do overlaps with the knowledge and skills they do not yet possess, even with help from a more competent other. The ZPD can be pictured like this (Figure 2.1):

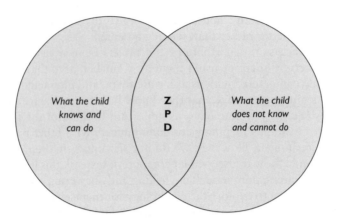

Figure 2.1 The zone of proximal development

Let's look at a practical example. A 3-year-old child does not require adult support to complete a task that they can do by themselves, such as building a simple tower using toy bricks. Indeed, adult help might even get in the way of achieving the goal of constructing the tower by frustrating them or leading them to lose interest. On the other hand, giving the same child a more complex task that they are unable to do, such as building a complicated model aeroplane, would be equally unhelpful because the task cannot be easily shared with the adult. The adult would have to do all of the task. The ZPD is the area in which tasks offer a sufficient challenge to the child, based on something with which they are already familiar. The adult has to take responsibility initially for some parts of the task, but the child is capable of doing at least some of it as it builds on existing knowledge or skills. Our 3-year-old might need some assistance to complete a 24-piece jigsaw puzzle, but they are already familiar with and competent at completing puzzles with 12 pieces. This basic knowledge will come in useful when attempting puzzles with a greater number of pieces.

As reading is a common task across all key stages and areas of the curriculum, we can use this as an example of how this applies in the classroom. If the focus for learning is on reading comprehension, the teacher may select a text which is challenging in terms of decoding for the child. The task can be shared, with the adult reading the text and the pupil answering the questions. If, on the other hand, the learning goal is to decode the words, the teacher may choose a less challenging text. But the text should have some words the pupil needs to practise and work out. If they could 'get the words off the page' too easily, it would not support them in extending their decoding skills.

The acquisition of new knowledge and skills – learning, in other words – occurs in the ZPD. It is the responsibility of teachers to plan tasks for pupils that fall within the space where the fringes of what a pupil knows and does not know overlap. So when a teacher plans a task, she will be thinking about which parts of a task the pupil can already do and what new things they are likely to learn by completing it. We have represented this on the grid below, using a maths task as an example.

Overall task: To calculate the amount of degrees in an angle under 180°		
Part of task	Things pupil can already do	Things pupil will learn during task
1 Make sure the protractor is the right way up (so you can read the numbers).	Choose the protractor from a range of resources. Put the protractor the right way up.	
2 Put the small circle of the protractor over where the two lines of the angle meet.	Put the circle over where the lines meet.	
3 Line up the thick line along the bottom of the protractor with the left hand line of the angle, making sure the circle stays in place.	Line up the two lines.	Reposition the protractor along the line so the little circle is in the correct place.
4 Starting from the left, use a pencil to follow the curve of the protractor, stopping where the right hand line of the angle is visible.	Follow the curve of the protractor.	
5 Using the numbers on the protractor, read off the angle.	Read off the large number (to the nearest 10).	Read off the whole number, so taking an accurate measure (counting along from nearest 10 in ones).

REFLECTION ACTIVITY

Think about a task that you have worked on with a pupil recently. Which parts of the task was the pupil able to do **when they started** the task? Which parts of the task did they learn to do **during** the task? Fill in the grid below.

Overall task:		
Part of task	Things pupil could already do	Things pupil learned during task
1		
2		

(continued)

(continued)

Overall task:		
Part of task	Things pupil could already do	Things pupil learned during task
3		
4		
5		

Applying social constructivist theory to the classroom

Social constructivist learning theory is of interest to people who work in education because it suggests that learning can be accelerated though interaction with others. A pupil can be introduced to new concepts, such as mathematical or scientific vocabulary, and skills, such as tying a shoelace or making a sandwich, by working on the task alongside an adult. The adult can allow the pupil to try parts of the task while they do the more challenging parts. As the pupil becomes more secure on the components of the task they can do successfully, they can be supported by the adult to attempt the more challenging parts. Eventually the child can try the task by themselves, checking their progress with the adult who is still close by.

Let's walk through an everyday example in more detail to show how the theory is applied in practice. From a young age, children enjoy watching an adult cook. If you observe closely, you will see the adult talking to the child, describing what they are doing step-by-step. After a time, the adult will let the child carry out parts of the cookery process that they can manage safely, such as pouring ingredients into a bowl or stirring a mixture. The adult will steady the jug or hold the bowl while the child stirs, responding to the fact that he can do part of the task, but not all of it; the young child might need all his strength to stir the mixture, so needs someone to hold the bowl. Over time, the child becomes more skilled at stirring, and physically stronger, so he will start to hold the bowl as well as stir. The child knows to do this because he has seen the adult doing it for him or heard them say 'I'll hold the bowl for you', and understands the significance of this part of the overall goal.

Making learning relevant

The goal in the example above is producing something nice to eat. The difficulty in the classroom is that children are often asked to do things in which they see no purpose.

What, they might ask, is the point of learning about life in Victorian Britain? Social constructivism relies on the pupil *wanting* to achieve a goal *because* they find meaning in the purpose behind it. This increases the likelihood that they will actively engage with others to help them achieve it. So it is really important that:

- the end goal of a task is made clear to the pupils;
- they see a purpose in learning how to achieve this goal and, wherever possible, there is some relevance to the 'real world';
- it is made clear how the task links to what they can already do, the knowledge and skills they bring to the task.

The teacher should do all of these things when planning tasks and during her whole-class teaching. It is important that in your role as a TA you are able to reinforce these points when interacting with pupils during the independent work part of the lesson.

REFLECTION ACTIVITY

Think about a task you have worked on with a pupil recently.

What was the end goal?

How did the learning link to 'real life'?

What knowledge and skills did the pupil bring to the task (e.g. what could they already do)?

The zone of learning

The ZPD is a useful way of thinking about developmental changes over time. However, even accepting that we can help quicken the pace of a pupil's cognitive development, it is still not going to happen during one session! It is the teacher's role to be aware of the overall development of the pupil and to plan tasks that move them forward at a suitable pace; their job requires having this broad view in mind.

But TAs working at the finer day-to-day, lesson-to-lesson level need not think about the overall cognitive development of the child. In your role, it is more helpful to take a task-level view; to know what skills or knowledge the pupil needs to have gained by the end of that *one* (teacher-planned) task. To do this successfully, it is important to know the 'mini-goals' the pupil needs to achieve during the task. Tasks are broken down into mini-goals, each of which marks a step towards a wider goal. So what you are focusing on is the progress towards achieving each mini-goal, during the task, rather than the child's broader development (Bickhard, 2005). You are already familiar with the concept of mini-goals, as these were the parts of the task referred to in the earlier example about using a protractor. We discuss mini-goals in more depth in Chapter 3.

Once you know the mini-goals that comprise a task, you can determine the mini-goal the pupil is working towards at each moment during the task, and whether and when it needs to change. For example, the pupil might need an even smaller mini-goal, or might be able to move through them more quickly. Although the teacher has planned the task, it will only ever be their best assessment of what the pupil will be able to do at that point in time. We can only be sure what a pupil can do or what they find difficult *during* the task. Careful observation and talking with the pupil – *interaction* – enables us to be more precise about what they actually know and are able to do. So learning is an interactive process. Both the TA and the pupil need to be actively engaged in the task and with each other. Neil Mercer (2000) calls this interaction the 'Intermental Development Zone' or 'zone of teaching-and-learning'. It is in this zone that scaffolding occurs.

Scaffolding

We will focus in detail on scaffolding in Chapter 3, but it is helpful to provide a brief introduction here as we continue to set the foundations for the rest of the book.

Scaffolding is the process by which learners are helped to achieve learning goals and to be able to carry out tasks independently. The term was first used by Wood, Bruner and Ross (1976) to describe the process of effective one-to-one tutoring. Since then, the idea has been applied more generally to other classroom contexts. Scaffolding can only be provided by a competent or skilled other; that is, someone who already knows how to achieve a given learning goal. As we made clear in Chapter 1, scaffolding is characterised by the way in which the competent person supports the learner by providing the least amount of help at any one point in the process. Three things are required for effective scaffolding in the classroom (Wood and Wood, 1996):

1   Close monitoring of the pupil's progress towards the part of the task being worked on.
2   Support which constantly adapts to the needs of the learner.
3   The gradual handover of responsibility and control of the task from the person doing the scaffolding to the pupil.

Collectively, we call these things *contingent teaching*.

In order to be able to scaffold successfully you need to know the overall goal of the task, the end 'product' (e.g. a sponge cake). You also need to know the smaller steps – or 'processes' – that must be completed successfully in order to achieve the end product (e.g. the stages that comprise the recipe's method). We call these smaller steps 'process success criteria' or, to use a now familiar term, 'mini-goals'. Mini-goals enable the person doing the scaffolding to monitor the progress the learner makes towards the end product or goal.

The scaffolder also needs to ensure that the learner is interested in the task in the first place by providing motivation, encouraging them to take risks and carefully managing any frustration they may experience. This can be particularly challenging with pupils who feel that they are not able to achieve as well as their peers or get worried or anxious if they are unable to get the task 'right' after the first attempt. We will return to this later in our discussion of 'mindsets'.

The purpose of scaffolding is to not just support the learner to complete a given task today, but ultimately to work towards the development of a 'mental toolkit' to enable the learner to carry out the same and similar tasks in the future by themselves. This is achieved through the process of the scaffolder handing over more and more responsibility for undertaking more and more of the task to the learner to complete independently. We consider scaffolding to be a key role for TAs. From our discussion so far, you can see that scaffolding is a very skilled process for which TAs with a pedagogical role should be properly trained and supported.

Classroom talk

The quality of the interactions that teachers and TAs have with children is the most important aspect of teaching and learning in the classroom. Clearly, the main way we interact with pupils is through talk, although other aspects of interaction, such as gesture, are also important for helping children learn. These, though, tend to supplement talk, rather than replace it.

As interaction is the key to learning, classroom talk has been the focus of a lot of research. This research has shown that there is a pattern to certain classroom talk which is not very helpful in supporting deep learning. This is known as the IRF pattern. IRF stands for:

Initiation   This is normally a question asked by the teacher. Usually one to which they already know the answer, such as 'What is the capital of Italy?'

Response   This is the pupil's answer. Let's say, in this case, the pupil's response is 'Paris'.

Feedback   This is the feedback the teacher provides on the pupil's answer. She will say whether the answer is right or wrong, and if it is wrong, why it is wrong. For example: 'No. Paris is the capital of France'.

Here is an example taken from a literacy intervention lesson with pupils aged 7 to 8 years old, where the TA has asked the group for the spelling of 'disgrace'.

I TA: Does anybody know how to spell it? Ryan.
R Ryan: Disgrass
F TA: Disgrace ... grace. As in the girl's name Grace.

REFLECTION ACTIVITY

The next time you are in the classroom, listen to the interactions that take place during the teacher's whole-class teaching. Note down some examples of the IRF pattern and, afterwards, reflect on the questions below.

Initiation	Response	Feedback

(continued)

(continued)

Initiation	Response	Feedback

What do you notice about the teacher's questions? Does he/she tend to use open questions or closed questions?

Was it clear from the teacher's response that he/she already knew the answer?

In his/her feedback move, does the teacher elaborate on why the answer is correct?

In his/her feedback move, does the teacher elaborate on why the answer is incorrect?

For incorrect pupil responses, can you detect where the pupil 'went wrong'?

The IRF pattern can be helpful in classroom contexts, but it does not always allow for the genuine collaboration between the learner and the adult. In our example above, the TA's feedback provides Ryan with something of a handy hint to help him spell 'disgrace', but she has missed an opportunity to unpick his response and work through *why* his answer is incorrect. As it is fairly clear whereabouts Ryan has gone wrong in his spelling, the TA could have used this information to improve the likelihood of Ryan not only spelling 'disgrace' correctly in the future, but also spelling other words that have a similar phonetic ending (e.g. replace or embrace). It is Ryan's understanding of the use of the word ending '-ace' that might be the wider problem here, not just having difficulty with a particular word.

Dialogic talk

'Dialogic talk' is an alternative technique that has been shown to be more effective than the IRF pattern of interaction. The term describes a genuine two-way discussion that builds shared understandings (Alexander, 2005). It is, therefore, very different from the

IRF pattern, where the pupil is guessing the answer already in the adult's head. Dialogic talk is similar to a concept called 'interthinking', which describes the 'use of language for thinking together, for collectively making sense of experience and solving problems' (Mercer, 2000, p. 1).

In dialogic talk, each participant has equal power and is expected to make contributions to the discussion. Martin Nystrand and his colleagues (1997) identified three key features of dialogic talk:

1 'Authentic questions': these are open questions to which the teacher may not know the answer, or to which there is more than one possible answer.
2 'Uptake': where responses are incorporated into subsequent questions.
3 'High level evaluation': this refers to the teacher's efforts to validate and elaborate on pupils' responses.

Let's illustrate these features of dialogic teaching in another example. The adult asks a child an open (authentic) question: 'What do you think it is like to visit Italy?' The child might respond by saying, 'They eat lots of pizza there'. The adult can then use the feedback move to build on what has just been said, rather than stating whether this is right or wrong (which it may or may not be!). In a dialogic talk uptake move, the adult might respond with the following: 'When I visited Italy I ate pizza too and lovely creamy ice-cream'.

Closed questions, which begin with phrases such as 'What is . . .', typically invite very short answers. This is also the case with questions to which the answer is just 'yes' or 'no'. And since answers do not develop very far, the topic changes quickly with each new IRF. For example, the adult might respond to the child's response about Italians eating a lot of pizza by asking 'Do you like pizza?'; another closed question that moves the topic of conversation from Italy to pizza. However, in dialogic talk, the child's answers tend to be longer and provide more information on which to maintain discussion on a specific topic. Achieving this relies on the adult validating and elaborating on the child's responses ('high level evaluation'). The collaboration between the adult and child sustains and extends the talk. For example, the child's next move in the example we have been discussing might be: 'Yes, I had ice-cream too when we had a ride on a gondola in Venice'.

Getting good at dialogic talk requires practice, but the effort is worthwhile. Innovative research led by Alexander, Mercer and Nystrand has shown that dialogic talk techniques are associated with improved learning outcomes and cognitive development. There are three key skills required for successful dialogic talk. They are:

Questioning   Asking authentic questions to find out a pupil's ideas about the part of the task they are doing.
Evaluating   Judging what to say next in response to what the pupil has just said.
Responding   Saying something which moves the pupil's thinking forward by building on what they have just said.

The following example is taken from a maths lesson in which Rob (who is 12-years-old) has just misread a question asking him to find out the mode. He asks a question to check the meaning with the TA:

Rob: What is the model?
TA: Model, model? What do you think that is?
Rob: Mode?
TA: Yes. What is mode anyway?

In this example, the TA starts by finding out more about what Rob thinks he has read: 'What do you think that is?' This prompts Rob to reflect on whether he read the word correctly. After reading the word again (this time correctly), he changes the word to 'mode'. The TA then extends Rob's thinking by asking a further question: 'What is mode anyway?' Importantly, the TA does not tell Rob that he has made a reading error or what mode means. Instead, the questions aim to get him to work out that he has misread a key component of the question, and to consider whether he knows what the word 'mode' means by drawing on his existing knowledge.

It can be challenging to introduce and maintain this type of classroom talk because both teachers and pupils have become so used to the IRF format. Traditionally, the teacher's role has been seen as 'transmitting' knowledge and asking questions that check whether pupils have remembered it. The pupil's role in this is to try and give the answer that the teacher is expecting. The IRF pattern exemplifies this way of teaching and learning, and it can increase the pace at which basic knowledge is exchanged. Yet, as we have seen, it is a technique that can miss out or bypass crucial opportunities for deeper learning.

As our research has shown, compared with teachers, TAs are often in the position of having extended opportunities to work with small groups or individual pupils. Therefore, you have greater opportunities to have longer conversations with pupils. These opportunities should be used to allow pupils to take an active and more equal part in conversations. TAs are in a prime position to use the dialogic talk strategies needed for effective scaffolding. We will describe the specific strategies in Chapter 4 and, as you will see, they all derive from the ideas we have discussed in this section.

REFLECTION ACTIVITY

Next time you are in the classroom, listen to the interactions that take place during the teacher's whole-class teaching. Note down some examples of dialogic talk and, afterwards, reflect on the questions below.

What do you notice about the teacher's questions? Did any of the questions start with open forms, such as 'How would . . . ?' or 'Why might . . . ?'

What did the pupils say in response?

Was it clear from the teacher's response that he/she already knew the answer?

Did any of the questions the teacher asked attempt to find out what the pupils were thinking? How were these questions worded?

Self-scaffolding

Scaffolding not only helps pupils to learn about the task they are doing there and then, but, as we noted earlier, has a broader purpose to help them to learn how to structure their own learning and how to think through similar tasks (Wood, 1988). So an overarching aim of scaffolding is to help pupils develop the skills of *self-scaffolding*. Self-scaffolding, also known as *metacognition*, describes your ability to:

* identify the goal and mini-goals;
* plan how to achieve each mini-goal;
* solve problems as you are working;
* review your progress towards mini-goals;
* evaluate your finished product and the effectiveness of your strategies.

Let's look at a practical example of a good 'self-scaffolder' in action. Courtney has been asked by her teacher to devise a demonstration to show water in its three states: as liquid, a solid and as vapour. Courtney has devised and conducted a demonstration before, so she uses what she already knows about scientific processes to work out that the task requires her to write down a list of equipment and instructions. Next, she breaks down the main task into three mini-goals. The first is to find a way to show water in its liquid state; the second mini-goal is to show it in solid form; and the third mini-goal is to find a way to show water as vapour. Courtney works out that showing water in liquid form is the easiest bit, as she can do this by pouring water from the tap into a beaker. To show water in solid form requires making ice, but waiting for the beaker of water to freeze will take a long time. So, to get around her problem, Courtney decides to start with the ice. She decides that she will melt the ice in a dish over the radiator in the classroom, thereby showing water turning from one state (solid) into another (liquid).

Courtney is initially a bit unsure of how to show water in vapour form; in fact, she is not certain she knows what vapour looks like. Courtney, though, is becoming an expert in 'knowing how to know'. So she Googles her question and soon gets her answer. Vapour is invisible, but the effects of vapour can be seen in the form of a white cloud or mist, such as the 'steam' from a boiling kettle. To show water in the third state, Courtney realises she will need to bring the water to boiling point in order to produce steam. To achieve this, she works out that she will need to transfer the water to a test-tube and hold it above the flame from a Bunsen burner. Having designed her demonstration, Courtney reviews her work and realises that by putting the ice over the Bunsen burner flame to melt it into liquid water, rather than using the radiator, she can speed up the time it takes to complete her demonstration and improve the efficiency of the whole operation.

Pupils who are able to self-scaffold, like Courtney, can work independently. But they also know when they need to ask for help. So, at any point in the example above, Courtney would know when and how to ask an adult for assistance so that she could carry on by herself. For instance, if she was unsure where she could obtain some ice on the school premises, she would know that an adult might be able to help her get some; perhaps from the freezer in the school kitchen. She also knows that she can use her peers as a source of help. So if the internet was not available, she could have asked another pupil what vapour is rather than looking it up.

Since self-scaffolding skills are learned through social interaction, children come into the schooling system with varying competency in this area. Children whose parents or carers have discussed with them how to approach tasks, solve problems and evaluate strategies are likely to have developed aptitude in these areas, and exhibit a willingness and capacity for independence. Children who have not had good-quality interactions with parents or carers, or have not been encouraged to try and think things through for themselves, will need support to develop self-scaffolding skills. Our research has led us to a clear conclusion that the TA role is potentially very important in achieving this for children who lack these fundamental life skills.

Whatever curriculum subject the pupil is working on, TAs are always able to work on developing pupils' self-scaffolding skills. TAs do not need to have expert subject or topic knowledge or know the specifics and intricacies of how to carry out the task. In these circumstances, scaffolding becomes a way of helping a pupil become familiar with the process of tackling problems, by introducing them to:

- How to approach a task – for example: reading instructions; reviewing information given by the teacher; collecting resources; and deciding what to do first.
- How to solve problems – for example: reflecting on similar tasks they have done (as with Courtney's experience of drawing on her existing knowledge of scientific processes and how to set up a demonstration); discussing with peers; accessing resources; and asking an adult.
- How to evaluate – for example: reviewing progress against mini-goals; thinking about how useful the strategies used were; and modifying work in light of this reflection.

We use the term *heuristic scaffolding* to refer to the way in which adults can help pupils to self-scaffold. Heuristic scaffolding supports the process of handing over responsibility and increasing pupils' capacity for independent thinking and working. The skills of effective questioning are essential for TAs because good-quality questioning can help pupils to talk about what they already know, how they are planning to approach a task and how they might try and solve problems. Often, giving the pupils you support the space and language to talk about their learning in real time is a key component of helping them to realise they have the capacity to self-scaffold just as effectively as anybody else. The following is an example of a TA using heuristic scaffolding strategies.

The TA is working with a group of 9- and 10-year-old pupils who have just watched a demonstration by the teacher of how to write a letter of complaint. They now have to think of something that they do not like about the school day and write a letter of complaint to the headteacher.

1	Chris:	What do I do?
2	TA:	What do you think you should do?
3	Chris:	Complain about something.
4	TA:	OK. So what do you want to complain about?
5	Chris:	So much!
6	TA:	So much! Right, well, that's a problem, isn't it? How are you going to choose something?
7	Chris:	I'm going to ask people which one they think is most important.
8	TA:	OK. What ones have they got to choose from?
9	Chris:	I'm going to make a list. Then I'll tick what they choose.

In line 2, the TA uses a standard response of 'What do you think you should do?' This is a good way of putting the responsibility for the task back on to Chris. It is clear from his response in line 3 that Chris does know what to do. The problem, as described by him in line 5, is that he cannot get started because he is unable to pinpoint what exactly he should choose to write about. In line 6, the TA highlights this as a problem (it is helpful to get pupils to recognise this) and asks him how he is going to solve the problem: 'How are you going to choose something?' Chris has a great idea in line 7 to carry out a survey. The TA helps move this forward in line 8 by asking a question which leads Chris to list the different possibilities.

REFLECTION ACTIVITY

Next time you are in the classroom, look for instances of pupils self-scaffolding. Note down some features of what pupils do to tackle problems by themselves. Afterwards, reflect on the questions below.

How effectively did pupils identify problems and break them down into mini-goals?

How effectively did pupils sequence these mini-goals into a plan?

Did pupils need to modify their plans as new problems arose? If so, how was this accomplished?

At what points in the task did the pupils turn to a peer for help?

At what points in the task did the pupils turn to an adult for help?

How did they ask the adult for help? Was there an expectation (or hope) that the adult would complete part of the task?

In your judgment, could they have done more by themselves before asking for help?

Mindsets

As the industrialist Henry Ford once said, 'Whether you think you can, or you think you can't, you're right!'. How we think about our own aptitudes and abilities has been shown to affect how we behave while we are doing a task – and even whether we will try it in the first place! Carol Dweck's (2012) extensive research has shown that there are (broadly) two types of mindset: fixed and growth.

People with a fixed mindset believe that intelligence is fixed and cannot be changed. These people believe and act as though they were born good or bad at a particular thing, which leads to them thinking that they will always be bad at some things and that trying to develop their skills in this area is likely to be a lost cause. Many people who struggle with maths, for example, will say that they have always found it difficult and they did not enjoy it or succeed with it at school. They claim that because they were never good at it, they never will be. This affects their confidence too, so having to engage with maths in real-world situations can induce a sense of anxiety over what feels like impending failure. People with a fixed mindset are reluctant to do tasks they think they might not achieve.

The other side of this coin is that people with a fixed mindset tend to undervalue the effort and practice that has helped them become an expert at something. They do not see their expertise as the result of hard work or learning, but as the result of natural talent. They will also view others in a similar light, attributing expertise to a 'gift' or a propensity for how their brain must be wired. Finally, they tend to place greater value on grades and outcomes than on the learning process.

People with growth mindsets believe that working hard at something makes you better at it. They are likely to adhere to the view that practice makes perfect. Although they might believe that they are naturally better at some things than others, they are willing to work hard to improve their skills in the areas that they find more challenging. They will keep going when they find things difficult, and are more interested in the process of learning and self-improvement than grades or outcomes. People with growth mindsets believe that learning itself is learnable, and that you can get better at it.

REFLECTION ACTIVITY

Do you have a fixed mindset or a growth mindset? What is your evidence for saying this?

Now think about the pupils that you work with. Can you think of one who has a fixed mindset? What is your evidence for this?

Can you think of one who has a growth mindset? What is your evidence for this?

Pupils with fixed mindsets can be successful and achieve in the education system, although they are very likely to struggle when they come across something they find particularly challenging or is outside their comfort zone; they are more likely to give up easily. They can become demotivated quickly if a subject they thought they were good at becomes more challenging for them, or if they are given negative feedback or a poor mark.

Pupils who are falling behind in their learning may develop more rigidly fixed mindsets because they see their lack of achievement as evidence that they are not good at those subjects. There are several ways through which their view of themselves as a learner becomes reinforced: with getting consistently lower grades than their peers; receiving feedback that they interpret as criticism; or not getting it right at the first or second attempt. These pupils can stop engaging with tasks and they fall further behind – all of which, as Henry Ford suggests, reinforces their fixed, underachieving mindset.

Pupils who have grown up with parents or carers who have fixed mindsets are likely to have learned the same ways of thinking. Pupils with growth mindsets are less likely to be affected by a single poor mark or become demotivated. Indeed, it can often be the spur to improve. The good news is that fixed mindsets are not as fixed as those that possess them might think. Adults can help pupils to develop growth mindsets by:

- focusing learning interactions on problem-solving, trying hard and valuing perseverance (keeping going when things become difficult);
- giving praise for persistence and effort, rather than scores or outcomes;
- talking about how you have learned to do something new or kept going when you have found something difficult.

You will notice that these things fit well with the concept and techniques of self-scaffolding. Working on developing self-scaffolding skills with pupils will help them to develop a growth mindset. Once pupils see they are able to work through problems and become more able to complete tasks independently, they will be motivated to continue to do this. Whatever else we desire from our education system, we can agree that these are valuable skills that all children and young people need to succeed, both in school and in life beyond it.

Summary

In this chapter, we have explained social constructivist learning theory as the basis for how we view the role of the TA. The key points we have covered are:

- The task must be within the pupil's zone of proximal development (ZPD).
- Learners must be actively involved in the task.
- The quality of the interaction between the TA and pupil can improve the pace and ease with which learning occurs.
- The role of the TA is to scaffold learning and help pupils develop a growth mindset.
- Dialogic talk techniques are important for effective scaffolding.
- The key skills of both dialogic talk and scaffolding are asking high-quality questions and providing feedback that builds on and extends the pupil's responses.
- When scaffolding, the TA needs to provide the least amount of support necessary at any one point in the process.
- Self-scaffolding needs to be taught and practised.

REFLECTION ACTIVITY

Review the ideas about learning theory that you made at the beginning of this chapter.

Have you changed any of your ideas?

Have you developed any new ideas?

Are there any ideas that we have discussed that remain unclear? How could you find out more?

References

Alexander, R. (2005) *Towards dialogic teaching: Rethinking classroom talk*. Cambridge: Dialogos.

Bakhtin, M. (1984) *Problems of Dostoevsky's poetics* (C. Emerson, Trans.). Minneapolis: University of Minnesota.

Bickhard, M. H. (2005) Functional scaffolding and self-scaffolding. *New Ideas in Psychology*, 23, pp. 166–173.

Bruner, J. (1983) *Child's talk: Learning to use language*. Oxford: Oxford University Press.

Dweck, C. (2012) *Mindset: How you can fulfil your potential*, tenth edition. London: Robinson. Available online at www.brainpickings.org/2014/01/29/carol-dweck-mindset/ (accessed 7 July 2015).

Mercer, N. (2000) *Words and minds: How we use language to think together*. London: Routledge.

Nystrand, M., Gamoran, A., Kachur, R. and Prendergast, C. (1997) *Opening dialogue: Understanding the dynamics of language and learning in the English classroom*. New York: Teachers College Press.

Piaget, J. (1977) *The origins of intelligence in the child*. Middlesex: Penguin Books.

Vygotsky, L. (1978) *Mind in society: The development of higher psychological processes*. Cambridge, MA: Harvard University Press.

Wood, D. (1988) *How children think and learn*. Oxford: Blackwell.

Wood, D. and Wood, H. (1996) Vygotsky, tutoring and learning. *Oxford Review of Education*, 22(1), pp. 5–16.

Wood, D., Bruner, J. S. and Ross, G. (1976) The role of tutoring in problem solving. *Journal of Child Psychology and Child Psychiatry*, 17, pp. 89–100.

Further reading

Lucas, B., Claxton, G. and Spencer, E. (2013) *Expansive education*. Milton Keynes: Open University Press.

Stobart, G. (2014) *The expert learner: Challenging the myth of ability*. Maidenhead: Open University Press.

Chapter 3

The principles of scaffolding

Having introduced the concept of scaffolding in the previous chapters, we will now discuss it in more detail. This chapter covers the idea of process success criteria (introduced in Chapter 2), which are key for identifying the things you might need to scaffold. Finally, ahead of more detailed coverage in Chapter 4, we introduce our framework for interaction to support you when scaffolding pupils' learning.

What is scaffolding?

'Scaffolding' is a term which is regularly used in educational discussions and in books, but is not often explained by those who use it. It gets used in different ways by different people, so as a result its meaning can lose clarity.

REFLECTION ACTIVITY

Have you heard the term scaffolding? If so, how would you define it?

Ask a few teachers how they would define scaffolding.

Ask your SENCO how he or she would define scaffolding.

(continued)

(continued)

What are the similarities and differences between the definitions?

Look at the answers to the questions in the activity above. The following words are likely to appear in the definitions you collected: help, support, differentiation, steps, breaking down, chunking down, structure, independence, contingent, talk, interaction. We would use some of these words when defining scaffolding, but we would avoid others.

Many of our discussions with teachers, SENCOs and TAs have suggested that scaffolding has become merged with 'help', 'differentiation' and 'support'. We do not think this is helpful, so we avoid using these words when describing scaffolding. To see why, we need to explain each of these in turn.

'Help' is a very general term that could mean anything from doing the task for a pupil, to providing a very small piece of information at the right time to assist their progression with the task. Help is not a specific enough term to describe what a TA needs to be doing when working with a pupil.

'Support' is often used interchangeably with help and is also a fairly non-specific term. We talk about adults working with children and young people to provide emotional support or behavioural support, as we did in our descriptions of the different types of TA roles at the start of this book. In terms of learning, we take support to mean anything that enables the pupil to access the task; so we rule out the kinds of help whereby the task is done for the child. Support might also take the form of resources, such as a writing frame or multilink blocks. These things can form part of a scaffolding approach but are not, in themselves, scaffolding.

'Differentiation' is the process of designing tasks appropriate for the learner. We looked at task design ideas in Chapter 2, where we discussed the importance of ensuring that the task is within the pupil's zone of proximal development. The key point here is that differentiation is done *before* scaffolding can take place.

So, if none of these terms describe scaffolding, what is it? In fact, it has a very specific meaning. Scaffolding was first used by Wood, Bruner and Ross (1976) to describe the way an adult can provide tuition to a pupil who is learning a new skill or concept. Scaffolding describes the ways adults provide *structured help*, so the pupil can reach a specific goal. As a TA, you are the adult providing structured help to individuals and groups. Until now, the educational world has not paid enough attention to the way we might apply the principles and practices of 'proper scaffolding' to the work of TAs.

The starting point is the task or activity, which should have been differentiated appropriately by the teacher. It is important that you do not change the task. Scaffolding is not about modifying the task, but simplifying what the pupil has to do in order to carry it out. So the adult *allows* the pupil to attempt each part of the task by herself, but provides structured help for the parts that she finds difficult. As the pupil becomes more skilled, she should be given more parts of the task to perform, until she can eventually perform all aspects independently.

The scaffolding process

Figure 3.1 shows the process of scaffolding.

Let's take an example of a common classroom task: handwriting. Lorelei is learning to form the lower case letter 't'. Alfie, the TA, provides a clear model of how to write the letter 't' correctly for Lorelei. He provides a tracing sheet with guide lines for her to follow and shows her how to use it. Alfie provides a verbal commentary which describes what Lorelei is doing as she writes, and this helps her to remember the finer stages of the process should she forget where she is. All of these things would be in stage 1. At stage 2, Lorelei improves. She uses the tracing sheet without Alfie showing her how. He provides less verbal commentary as she takes on more responsibility for remembering each step of the process. Instead, Alfie asks Lorelei questions to prompt her to remember what to do next. The amount of support that Alfie gives will fade significantly during stages 1 and 2. Fading is the gradual withdrawal of support given to the pupil when it is no longer needed. At stage 3, Lorelei can write a lower case 't' independently, competently and with confidence.

It is important that you monitor how much the pupil is able to do, or is confident to try for themselves, and step back to allow them to attempt tasks independently. This can be difficult to do, particularly if you are assigned to work with a pupil on a one-to-one basis, or if the pupils you work with have become used to high levels of support. It is very important to withdraw, because if TAs provide too much support or do too much of the task for the pupil, the likelihood of them becoming dependent on adult support increases. As pupils routinely outsource their learning to the readily available TA, the chances of them developing independence greatly reduce. They will become stuck at stage 1, never trying the parts of the task that they find more difficult.

Some pupils require a lot of support initially, but you need to consciously withhold support to see if they are able to do more by themselves. Stepping back helps to move them into stage 2. You can always offer an additional scaffolding strategy if they struggle. To use the handwriting example from earlier, if Alfie noticed that

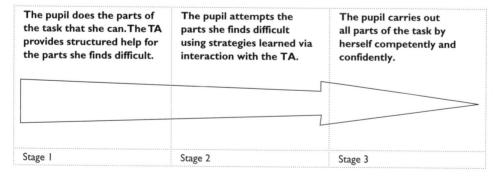

The pupil does the parts of the task that she can. The TA provides structured help for the parts she finds difficult.	The pupil attempts the parts she finds difficult using strategies learned via interaction with the TA.	The pupil carries out all parts of the task by herself competently and confidently.
Stage 1	Stage 2	Stage 3

Figure 3.1 The scaffolding process

Lorelei was having difficulty forming the letter 't' at stage 2, he might prompt her with a question, such as: 'What could you use to help you make your t's?' This places the responsibility on Lorelei to think of what might help her: a tracing sheet, thinking back to Alfie's commentary, or talking herself through the action of writing a 't'.

This means that there will be times when you are not actively 'helping' pupils. But this does not mean that you are not doing your job! In fact, an effective TA is one who is *not* constantly interacting with pupils. Instead, they are allowing them to try things for themselves, observing their progress, and only intervening for a specific reason. Giving pupils space to try things and praising their efforts, whatever the outcome, supports them to develop the growth mindset that they need to succeed in the long term.

If stages 1 to 3 are completed successfully, then the pupil will have assumed responsibility for the whole task and be able to carry it out confidently and to a sound level of mastery. Once the pupil has taken responsibility for completing the activity, they will be able to self-scaffold when adults are not at hand; for example, by asking themselves: 'I'm not sure what to do next. How can I find out?' These are actions that, with practice, develop even greater levels of independence, of course with the option of 'checking' with the adult if really needed.

We are often asked how long it takes for a child to progress through the stages, but this depends on the complexity of the task and the needs of the pupil. The gap between stage 1 and stage 3 might be five minutes, half a lesson or several lessons (depending on the needs of the learner). The important thing is that you are clear that the pupil can and will take responsibility for all parts of the task, and you are constantly encouraging and nudging them towards this.

Contingency

Accepting that pupil responsibility is the basis for effective scaffolding, we can now add another important ingredient. 'Contingency' is the act of responding moment-by-moment to what the pupil has just done or said. This involves asking diagnostic questions so that you can judge what a child knows and can do. If we take our handwriting example once more, the open questions that the TA could ask include:

- 'Where do you put your pencil first?'
- 'Which direction will you move it in?'
- 'What are you going to do next?'

Questions like these can be helpful in finding out what the pupil knows and can do. The feedback that you get from the pupil (the answers they give you) can help you to decide how much support you need to give for different parts of the task. At all times, you need to be thinking: 'What is the least amount of help that I can give?' You can always give more help if it is needed, but you must start with the least possible amount. So, if the child does not know how to describe the direction they need to move the pencil in, you might say: 'You start to move it and then tell me'. If the child is still having difficulty, you might then say: 'You move your pencil and I will describe what you are doing'.

Contingency highlights how fine-grained the process of good scaffolding is. Every move matters. We will be exploring particular scaffolding strategies later, and looking at them in more detail in Chapter 4. What is important is that you ask well-timed and appropriate diagnostic questions and observe the progress of the pupil during the task. These are your cues for calibrating the amount and type of support you give. This is what contingency means.

Observing and listening to children's responses carefully and applying appropriate talk strategies in response are learnable skills. The better we become at these things, the more likely it is the answers from pupils, on which we build our responses, will grow in quality. Eventually, pupils will be able to ask and answer these questions for themselves, and will have developed the internal monologue that defines self-scaffolding.

So scaffolding can *only* be provided through interaction. This is why it is not the same as differentiation or loosely qualified terms like 'help' and 'support', which do not necessarily involve adult–pupil interaction.

REFLECTION ACTIVITY

Review the definitions of scaffolding that you gathered. How far do they match our definition?

Process success criteria

Before you can scaffold pupils' learning, you need to know what you are aiming for and how you will know that the task is being carried out successfully. Success criteria are the key to this. Shirley Clarke (2014) has written a great deal about success criteria and we have used her concept of process success criteria (or mini-goals) to underpin our framework.

The success criteria that are often used in classrooms relate to the *product*: the thing – usually tangible, like a piece of writing – that must be produced. These will often be provided (or developed with the pupils) as a list at the beginning of the lesson. For example, if the task was to describe the properties of 2D shapes, the success criteria might be that pupils need to:

- name the shape;
- say how many sides the shape has;
- say how many vertices the shape has;
- say how many right angles the shape has.

This list will be used at the end of the lesson for pupils to self-assess against. Product success criteria tend to get used because the teacher usually only has the product to consider when marking. This leads to the selection of success criteria which is driven by the need for a written product.

However, when you are working with a small group or an individual you can observe the *process*; that is, *how* the child is doing the task. As we have said before, TAs get to do this more than teachers, so it is essential that TAs know: a) how to interact with pupils in these situations, and b) how to provide teachers with information about how pupils are doing (more of which later).

Process success criteria are more useful as they provide a greater understanding of exactly what a pupil can do in relation to an activity. As process success criteria might not be seen in the finished product, the teacher may not see it in the work she is marking. However, these criteria can help to demonstrate that a pupil has made progress, even if it is not detectable in the finished task. Put another way, setting and working towards product success criteria means that we can fail to record and respond to important steps of the learning journey.

Let's think about the success criteria in the example above. In response to the question, 'How many sides does a square have?', Ranee has written in her book the answer '5'. Later that day, when marking her work against the product success criteria, Ranee's teacher sees that she does not know that a square has four sides. Having not spent any time with Ranee during the lesson, he has little idea of *why* she had written '5'. There are several possibilities: has Ranee misnamed the shape; has she miscounted when counting up the sides; or does she not know what a 'side' is, so had a guess? All the teacher would know from marking her book is that this product is incorrect. He has no feedback in relation to what he needs to do next to help Ranee, if indeed she needs help, because her answer may be the result of an honest mistake.

Process success criteria take the overall task goal (the product) and split it into the different steps needed to achieve that goal. Process success criteria are all the steps or elements required in order to complete the task successfully. Each step is a 'mini-goal'. In order to scaffold effectively, you need to be clear about each mini-goal (exactly what they are), so that you can assess how much the pupil is able to do in relation to each one. Consider the protractor task in Chapter 2. Learners need to know and understand what these mini-goals are and have feedback *as they work* about their progress towards each one in turn.

REFLECTION ACTIVITY

Let's take an everyday example from outside the classroom. You are, no doubt, an expert at making sandwiches and have made hundreds over the years. So, imagine going into your kitchen to make a cheese sandwich: this is your overall task goal.

> *Write down every step that you would take to make your cheese sandwich. Define each step as a mini-goal; these are your process success criteria.*

We are also experts at making cheese sandwiches! Below are our steps to making one, written as mini-goals:

1   Wash your hands.
2   Take two slices of bread.
3   Butter one side of each slice with a knife.
4   Slice the cheese with a sharp knife.
5   Place the slices of cheese on one of the buttered sides.
6   Place the other slice of bread, buttered side down, on top of the cheese.
7   Slice the sandwich in half with a knife.

You may have written more than seven steps, or fewer. The precise number of steps is not what is important here; look at the language that we used. You will notice that each of our process success criteria starts with a verb. This is very important as it makes the action the mini-goal describes *observable*. This means you can watch or listen to the pupil demonstrating that they can do that mini-goal. This is why *process* success criteria are very different from *product* success criteria.

To use the sandwich example, a teacher looking at a cheese sandwich produced by a child some time after the event would be unable to judge whether some of the processes involved had been met. For example, did the pupil wash their hands; is it possible to tell just by looking at the finished sandwich? The teacher would also be unable to tell how much support the child had with each mini-goal. For example, did the child slice the cheese or did someone else do it for them? The teacher would still be unsure to what extent the child has developed cheese-cutting skills. A TA working with the pupil would have been able to observe whether the child had carried out each mini-goal independently, and record it on behalf of the teacher.

The cheese sandwich example is quite straightforward because it is a practical task. We have found that it is easier to produce mini-goals for practical tasks, where the overall process can be broken down into a clear set of sequenced steps. Also, with such fine-grained steps, there is little or no room for confusion or variation in how the task can be approached; there are only so many ways one can butter a slice of bread! It is much harder to think through goals for more abstract tasks or tasks that do not have a linear set of steps. Try the task below because it is an example that we are more likely to see in the classroom: writing an account of a school trip.

REFLECTION ACTIVITY

Write down all the process success criteria required to write about a school trip. Define each mini-goal that a pupil would need to do in order to produce an account of a school trip.

You will probably have found this more difficult to think about, compared with the cheese sandwich exercise. Having some subject knowledge is important here, as you need to know the features of a recount text. Your response to the school trip activity is likely to have covered key skills such as: state the key events; put the events in chronological order; and write using the past tense. You would have picked up this information by tuning into the teacher's talk, though for a relatively straightforward task like writing about a school trip, it is likely you will know what the key skills are anyway. However, there are tasks for which you will find the processes more complex to identify, depending on your own subject knowledge. This is why we argue that it is important for TAs to have the opportunity to discuss their role in lessons with teachers beforehand. At the very least, TAs need to be present for the teacher input part of the lesson, as this is when the teacher will explain the process(es) that the pupils will need to follow, and give the key skills to be developed or practised.

It is important that you are clear about each different part of the task (the mini-goals). The teacher you are working with should provide you with the process success criteria before the lesson, but we know – and our research confirms – that even with the best intentions, this is not always possible. So in such circumstances, you should use the time when the teacher is giving the whole-class input and explanation of the task to draft a list of process success criteria. You can check these with the teacher at a suitable break in the lesson, when the teacher has finished their input and the children are settling at their tables.

REFLECTION ACTIVITY

Think of two recent lessons and the tasks you were asked to support pupils with. List the process success criteria for these two tasks.

Task 1

Task 2

Discuss the lists with the teacher(s) who set the tasks. What are their thoughts on your lists?

Your role when working with pupils, individually or in groups, is to determine which process success criteria each pupil can complete independently, and which require adult intervention. Later, we will look at the different levels this intervention can take, but for now let's take a very straightforward example. One of the first things pupils need to be able to do when they start school is to hang up their coat in the correct place. This task can be split into the following process success criteria, which we have couched in terms of the steps the pupil might say aloud to themselves:

What do I need to do when I come inside? Hang my coat up. So I have to:

1   Find the coat rack.
2   Find the correct peg.
3   Hang my coat up on the peg.

Initially the pupil might have each step *modelled* by a TA, who will tell them that they need to hang their coat up, take them to where the coat racks are and show them how to hang up their coat. The next day the adult might ask the pupil what they need to do when they come in. If they remember that they need to hang up their coat, but cannot remember where, then the adult might:

• ask them if they can point to where the coats are;
• ask them to look at what the other children are doing;
• ask them if there is someone they could ask to help them (the preferred answer here is another child).

You will have noticed that the TA has avoided simply telling or showing the child what to do. Instead, the TA uses scaffolding strategies that offer a partial clue or hint to help the child think for themselves. You can probably think of other scaffolding strategies that might be used. The key thing is that the adult must try to avoid taking them to the coat area again unless it is clear that the child really cannot find it independently, or with help from a peer. The same principle applies when using any process success criteria. The role of the TA, remember, is:

• to let the pupil attempt to complete each mini-goal independently;
• to provide the least amount of support first, when intervening;
• to withdraw support as soon as possible to allow independent work.

REFLECTION ACTIVITY

Look back at the previous exercise in which you developed process success criteria.

Which of the processes did the pupil(s) take responsibility for initially?

Which of the processes did the pupil(s) take least responsibility for initially? (You may have ended up completing this step.)

Which processes did the pupil(s) take more responsibility for as the task progressed?

Remember: each process success criterion is a mini-goal. The pupil will need to know what the goal is and to have specific feedback on their progress towards this goal *as they work*. This is an essential part of the contingency working we have described; the feedback you give is contingent on what the pupil has just done or said.

As children become more skilled and confident, they will need less feedback and less frequently. In order to do this, and to move to stage 3 – full independence – pupils need the skills of being able to judge their own progress towards goals. We will cover this aspect of scaffolding in Chapter 5.

A summary of scaffolding

Before we conclude this chapter, a brief summary of the key features of scaffolding is helpful. So, scaffolding:

- happens only through interaction;
- relates to the specific mini-goal (process success criteria) that the pupil is working on;
- happens in the moment, in response to what the pupil has just said or done;
- is informed by careful observation, diagnostic questioning and asking the pupil to 'talk aloud' as they work;
- can be more accurate and precise as more detailed information about the strategies the pupil is using becomes available;
- relies on encouraging pupils to ask and answer the question 'what do I do next?' effectively and routinely;
- is defined by giving the least amount of support and consistently ensuring that the pupil takes as much responsibility for the task as they can.

REFLECTION ACTIVITY

Think about your own practice and interactions with pupils. Given what we have discussed so far, is there anything you might change about what you do?

How can the teachers and TAs you work with help you to achieve these changes? Discuss your ideas with your colleagues.

A scaffolding framework for TA–pupil interaction

The majority of the early work on scaffolding was done in relation to adults interacting with individual children in a parent role in informal contexts, or in a more formalised 'tutor' role, like a school teacher. In everyday classrooms, however, the opportunities for sustained one-to-one teacher–pupil interaction are often very limited. Research on classroom interactions suggests only 3 per cent of pupils' interactions are of this kind; less than two minutes for every hour in the classroom (Webster, 2015).

It would not be possible for a teacher working with a class of 30 pupils to effectively scaffold learning for each of them, bearing in mind that the starting point and potential for independence for any one learner will be different and will vary with every activity. However, when TAs are deployed effectively, they are in a prime position, working with groups and individuals, to scaffold learning in the way we have discussed. So what strategies can you use to do this?

Figure 3.2 shows our scaffolding framework, which we have used to structure our guidance on how TAs can interact with pupils.

At the top of the framework is self-scaffolding, which offers the highest level of pupil independence. At the bottom of the framework is correcting. Correcting offers no pupil independence because the adult is doing all the work. Below, we introduce each layer of the framework and, to provide some illustration, we will use the example of a task of writing an argument for or against school uniform. This will help to show what each of these levels of scaffolding looks like in practice.

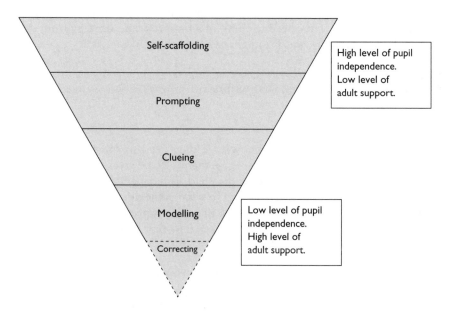

Figure 3.2 Scaffolding framework

Self-scaffolding

A pupil who is able to self-scaffold is an independent learner. Self-scaffolding can also be called self-regulated learning. This is our aim for *all* pupils. Pupils able to self-scaffold can:

- plan how to approach a task;
- problem-solve during the task;
- review the success of the task and how they approached it.

Self-scaffolders who are writing their arguments about school uniform are able to:

- write a list of the advantages and disadvantages of having a school uniform (as a planning tool);
- write whether they agree or disagree with having school uniform;
- provide reasons for their argument, with relevant examples;
- give counter-arguments, for balance;
- write about why they do not agree with the counter-arguments.

Prompting

Prompting represents the first level of adult intervention, when a pupil is unable to self-scaffold their way to the accomplishment of a mini-goal. Providing a prompt means saying or doing something to encourage the pupil to draw on their own knowledge of what to do when they do not know what to do. Saying nothing is a useful prompt, as extra thinking time is sometimes all that is needed. If this does not work, you need to say something which encourages the pupil but does not give any idea of the strategy they need to use. They need to think of an appropriate strategy from the ones they know. In our example, the TA might say something like:

- 'What do you need to do first?'
- 'What's your plan for structuring your writing?'

Clueing

Sometimes pupils have the strategies or knowledge they need to solve the problem locked in their minds, but find it difficult to access them. A clue gives the pupil a hint in the right direction and puts them back on the road to independence. As we have described it, clueing sounds a bit like prompting; so what is the difference? Think of it this way: a prompt means getting a pupil to think of an appropriate strategy; a clue is a means of getting a pupil to think of a *particular* strategy that you know they know. So, in our example, a clue would sound like:

- 'What did the teacher do before she started her writing?' *The answer is write a list of advantages and disadvantages.*
- 'Do you agree or disagree with having a school uniform? Why?' *The answer will provide the structure for the first section of writing.*
- 'You have said that not wearing school uniform is more expensive. How much more expensive are normal clothes?' *The answer provides an example.*

Modelling

When a skill or strategy is completely new to a pupil, it is helpful to have it modelled by someone who is confident in this area. Depending on the task, pupils might be given step-by-step instructions to support them in practising a skill or strategy, thereby reducing the need for adult help. In our example, the TA might say:

- 'Have a look back at the board. What has the teacher written on there?' *There is a model of an advantages/disadvantages list on the board.*
- 'Look at the list of instructions. You have done number 1. What does number 2 say?' *This models how to follow a list of instructions to complete a task.*

Correcting

Correcting is simply providing the right answer or completing the task for the child. This requires no independent thinking on the part of the child and is to be strenuously avoided. TAs operating within this layer of the framework can (as it were) 'put words into the pupil's mouth', and so give the pupil the next sentence they could write. So, in our example, the TA might say:

- 'So, you have said you don't like having school uniform. Is that because it isn't very fashionable?'

Sometimes a TA response might sound like a correction but is actually working as a model. For example:

TA: You have said that you don't like having school uniform. Why not?
Pupil: Not very fashion.
TA: It is not very fashionable? OK, so you can give that as a reason, can't you?

The TA's response ('It is not very fashion*able*') might be considered as correcting the pupil's response, but it is actually working as a language model by stressing the suffix required for the answer to make sense. Models such as this are very important. For example, pupils learning English as an Additional Language, or with speech and language needs, will need to have language modelled a great deal. The key is in knowing whether the pupil would be able to self-correct if prompted or if they need a correct model to be given.

Summary

In this chapter, we have discussed the concept of scaffolding in some detail, providing the precise definition that we have used as the basis for this book. It should now be clear why we see the term 'scaffolding' as a more useful way of explaining the way TAs should interact with pupils, compared with harder to pin down terms such as 'help' and 'support'. We have looked at contingency as a trigger for interactions, and given much thought to how we phrase and sequence *process* success criteria, and why it is helpful to choose these over product success criteria. We have also introduced a framework to support your scaffolding interactions with pupils. We will explore the layers of this framework in much more detail in Chapter 4.

References

Clarke, S. (2014) *Outstanding formative assessment: Culture and practice*. Abingdon: Hodder Education.

Webster, R. (2015) The classroom experiences of pupils with special educational needs in mainstream primary schools – 1976 to 2012. What do data from systematic observation studies reveal about pupils' educational experiences over time? *British Educational Research Journal*. Available online at: http://maximisingtas.co.uk/assets/content/berj35 sysobs.pdf (accessed 7 July 2015).

Wood, D., Bruner, J. S. and Ross, G. (1976) The role of tutoring in problem solving. *Journal of Child Psychology and Child Psychiatry*, 17, pp. 89–100.

Chapter 4

Scaffolding strategies

In Chapter 3, we discussed the TA as a scaffolder of learning. This role has benefits for all pupils, regardless of whether they have learning needs. To briefly recap, scaffolding starts from having a clear set of process success criteria (or mini-goals) which have been specified by the teacher. From here, the TA scaffolds learning through:

- careful observation: watching and listening to what the pupil is doing;
- asking diagnostic questions to check the pupil's understanding;
- providing structured help: a targeted response designed to move the pupil forward and ensure they retain responsibility for the learning, and that they do as much as possible independently.

In this chapter, we will explore specific strategies you can use to monitor and respond to pupils' actions during tasks. Throughout this chapter, we have used 'real-world' examples taken from our own research and professional development work with TAs in schools in order to illustrate particular strategies.

Preparation

When you are in the classroom, it is helpful, before the task starts, to think about the process success criteria that comprise the overall task. You can do this by asking some specific questions.

Which of the process success criteria:

- Can the pupil already do?
- Might need a resource to support the pupil to achieve it? If so, do they know how to use it?
- Might need interactional support? This is likely if they know how to use a technique or strategy, and/or have had it modelled, but they might need further prompts or clues to remind them.
- Are new to the pupil? If so, they may need to be modelled.

Working through these questions will help you to anticipate which parts of the task the pupil should be allowed to complete independently, which parts you need to observe, but resist intervening in, and which parts you will need to be involved in.

REFLECTION ACTIVITY

Choose a task you will be working on with an individual pupil or a group and complete the details below. If you are working with a group, you will need to work through the questions and provide a response for each individual.

Task goal:

Process success criteria (number them):

1

2

3

4

Which of the process success criteria can the pupil already do?

Which of the process success criteria might need a resource to support the pupil to achieve it? If so, do they know how to use it?

Which of the process success criteria might need interactional support? This is likely if they have had the process modelled and/or performed it before, but it is not secure.

Which process success criteria are new to the pupil? If so, will they need to be modelled?

A framework for interactions during the task

We designed the framework introduced in Chapter 3 (Figure 3.2, repeated below) to help TAs think about how they interact with pupils. It is intended for use as you work with pupils because, as we saw in the last chapter, it is this 'real-time' feedback on what they are saying and doing that is so valuable to their learning and the development of self-scaffolding skills.

In broad terms, you must always start at the top of the triangle, with the expectation that the pupil will scaffold their own learning. You intervene at the moments when the pupil experiences a difficulty they cannot overcome by themselves. At this point, it should be clear that some form of adult-led interaction is required.

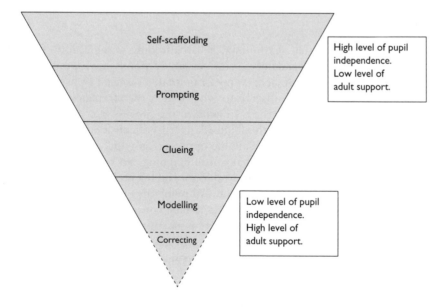

The framework is based on the principle that the adult-led strategies increase in the amount of help offered as you move down each layer of the triangle. Remember: you should work to the rule of providing the *least* amount of help first. You need to use the strategies associated with one layer of the model before moving down to the next layer. At all times, avoid correction and hopping between strategies within each layer.

Within each layer of the framework, there is a range of strategies you could use. In this sense, whilst the movement through the layers is fixed, there is flexibility *within* each layer. Your choice of the appropriate strategy will be determined by a number of things, including:

- what the pupil has just said or done;
- your awareness of the knowledge and skills the pupil brings to the task (e.g. learning from previous lessons);
- your knowledge of the pupil's level of self-confidence and their ability to take risks and cope with setbacks.

This last point is important. It might indicate that we should provide a higher level of support for pupils who find it harder than others to cope with the setbacks that accompany learning; but this is not the case. It might, though, change your interactions around a specific task in the short term. For example, you might provide more clues to support the pupil to succeed, even if you think they could with just a prompt, if pushed. The point is to use such techniques carefully and sparingly in service of the long-term aim of developing their independence. We must actively avoid creating a sense in pupils' minds that you are there to do the task (or most of it) for them. Always discuss with the teacher how support will be faded out over time.

The rest of this chapter contains practical suggestions and ideas on what to do in your moment-by-moment interactions with pupils. We now work through each section of the framework, starting with self-scaffolding.

Self-scaffolding

At the top of the framework is self-scaffolding. Self-scaffolding is the ability to be able to work through tasks independently, using strategies pupils have previously learned to help themselves. Your role here is quite minimal. You need to listen very carefully to what the pupil says and observe to what extent the strategies they are using are effective in terms of helping them to achieve the process success criteria. You can also use the observation time to think ahead in terms of considering how you will intervene (if the need arises) and the available options (e.g. which strategies you could use). TAs we have worked with say that not intervening can be very challenging. This is understandable. It can be uncomfortable to watch a child struggle, as we have to fight against our urge to ease the situation. Allowing the pupil to self-scaffold requires you to set your own anxieties to one side, which can indeed be difficult at first. The thing to remember is that the struggle is an essential part of the learning process. Through your on-going observations, you will get familiar with the signs that signal when your support is needed. Periods of struggle are always limited and your intervention will be timed to ensure that the pupil does not get upset unnecessarily or completely disengage through frustration.

Self-scaffolding involves:

- planning how to approach a task;
- problem-solving during the task;
- reviewing our success at the task and the strategies we used.

We will now take each of these in turn and describe what self-scaffolding looks like and how we can support the development of skills needed for effective planning, problem-solving and review.

Planning how to approach a task

How many times have you been in a classroom, listened to the teacher explain the task to the class, then, once sent to their tables to work, have a pupil ask you, 'What are we doing?' Maybe you have supported pupils who sit without doing anything until you tell them the first step. Both of these situations are strongly suggestive of pupils not taking ownership of their learning and relying too heavily on you to fill in the blanks.

As will be clear by now, you have a critical role to play in not only breaking this habit, but in supporting the development of far more productive learning habits. We want pupils to be able to identify and take the steps they need to complete a task, having been given clear instructions by the teacher. This is what self-scaffolding looks like.

Instructions from the teacher might be verbal or written, or a mix of both. In order to plan the task from written instructions, self-scaffolders need to identify steps using the information provided. The first step tends to be the hardest. Often it is getting ready to start the task that distracts pupils most. Prompt sheets reminding pupils of typical first steps can help. Here is an example:

- Collect all of the equipment that you need.
- Write the date.
- Write the title.
- Read the instructions.
- Identify what you need to do first.

This kind of prompt sheet can be adjusted for the age of the pupil and how your school/teacher works. It means, however, that at the very start of a task, the pupil should be expected to work through each step on the prompt card before they seek help from you.

It is harder if the instructions have been delivered verbally rather than in writing. In this case, some things that can help are the following:

- Allow the pupil to take notes in a form which is helpful to them, while instructions are given.
- Use an audio recorder to record instructions so that the pupil can play them back. The pupil can be given the responsibility for using the recorder.

- Ask the pupil to recall the steps needed and write down the steps and any keywords.
- Use a picture board to show key steps (e.g. drawing, cutting, gluing). This could include using symbol systems like Makaton.

Problem-solving during the task

Some pupils only have one strategy for solving problems as they work through a task. That strategy is to ask the TA! Other children have a different strategy: do nothing and wait for an adult to notice that they need help. For some pupils, these strategies have proved to be quite successful, but they are not consistent with what we expect from self-scaffolders. A self-scaffolding pupil will have strategies they can use before they seek help from you. These might include:

- carefully re-reading the instructions, their notes or text relating to the task;
- using a resource within the classroom, such as information on a display, a dictionary or thesaurus, a number line, multilink blocks or even the internet;
- reviewing previous work in their books;
- talking to a peer;
- asking the teacher. It is important that pupils know that they can ask the teacher. Pupils that have routine support from a TA often think that this is not the case.

Again, these strategies can be put on to a prompt card to remind pupils of the self-scaffolding strategies that are available to them, before asking you. Cards can be tailored to suit the particular needs of pupils, so the wording might be adjusted or symbols or pictures added. We even know one primary school that has the 'helpful hen': a classroom display with doors to open and which reveal strategies pupils can use if they are stuck.

Research has shown that, when a pupil has a TA close at hand, it is more likely they will ask them for help with things that they could do independently (Giangreco, 2010). If you can physically withdraw during the parts of the task pupils can work on independently, it encourages them to self-scaffold and think for themselves. In such instances, we recommend that you stealthily keep an eye on their progress, so you can provide support, if it is needed.

In some cases, it might not be desirable to withdraw entirely. For example, a pupil might need the reassurance of having you nearby as a part of a temporary strategy to aid anxiety. In such circumstances, it can be helpful to sit nearby doing another activity, such as making resources. Just observing can inadvertently add to any pressure the child may feel to quickly produce a response to the task, and may encourage them to engage with you when it is not necessary. So keeping busy with another activity is likely to result in pupils trying self-scaffolding techniques before they interrupt you.

Reviewing the success of the task and the strategies used

Once the task is completed, a good self-scaffolder will be able to identify which parts of the task they were successful in completing, which they found challenging and what they would do differently next time. Having clear process success criteria helps pupils to identify their progress against the different parts of the task.

We shall return to this in Chapter 5 when we discuss assessment for learning.

Putting this into practice

Let's think about the task we discussed in Chapter 3: writing arguments for or against having school uniform. Depending on the part of the task, the following self-scaffolding strategies could be applied. Remember: the key to a good strategy is that it is at a relatively general level, so it can be applied to similar situations (e.g. writing an argument on another topic):

- Write a list of advantages and disadvantages. Remember to use keywords.
- Put the items in order of importance.
- Group items that might be related (e.g. by colour-coding).
- Draft the content of each paragraph using the items on the list.
- Cross off each item on the list as it is written about.
- Make a list of vocabulary needed for persuasive writing (e.g. but, so, therefore, of course, firstly).
- Look at a previous example of persuasive writing for vocabulary and sentence starters.
- Look at the example(s) of an opening paragraph modelled by the teacher.
- Ask peers for examples of how to provide evidence for arguments.
- Read ideas to a peer and invite them to provide a counter-argument. Note what they say.

These are just some of the self-scaffolding strategies that could be used in many tasks and across many curriculum subjects and topics. You will be able to think of many other examples. As you do, bear in mind that the strategies above read like process success criteria, with each mini-goal starting with a verb. This is quite deliberate because, in many ways, self-scaffolding *is* the ability to set your own mini-goals, in service of accomplishing an overall task.

It is worth noting too that the strategies above can form the basis of prompts or clues you can use to scaffold pupils towards independence.

Prompting

The reason that some pupils cannot or do not self-scaffold is because they cannot understand or do the task. It has happened to all of us at some point in our school career, and very often more than once. Most of us will recall a task where we just could not understand what the teacher was explaining. That most of our classmates seemed to get it and be able to proceed with the task would probably have given rise or added to our negative feelings.

For some pupils, the first reaction to being presented with a new concept or complex information relating to a task can be confusion or even mild panic. This, of course, impedes their ability to think clearly. It is important to remember that, because the task has been planned to be within the zone of proximal development, the starting point will have some basis in their prior knowledge – even if it is not clear to them at first what that prior knowledge is! It can take time for some pupils to realise that there are elements of the task that are similar to something they have done before, and this information might need to be teased out.

Therefore, if a pupil is unable to self-scaffold their way towards a particular process success criterion, you can move to the next step on the framework and intervene with a prompt. A prompt is an action – something you might say or gesture you might give – that is designed to encourage the pupil to draw on their prior learning.

There are three types of useful prompts: saying nothing, verbal prompts and gesture.

Saying nothing

We have observed the following situation in dozens of classrooms, which brings home the importance of giving pupils time to think. The teacher asks the class a question. There is a momentary hush, indicating that the pupils are contemplating the question. The silence is broken, perhaps only a few seconds after the teacher has asked the question, by a TA asking the pupil(s) she is sitting with, 'What do you think?'

In the situation above, the supported pupils have less time to ponder the question, relative to their classmates, because the TA has cut in too early. It is important to remember that waiting time is essential to provide thinking time for pupils; and some pupils will need more thinking time than others. As we discussed above, TAs need to resist the temptation to say or do something.

It might seem counterintuitive, but sometimes the best thing to do is nothing. This allows pupils the necessary time and space to think *without pressure*. The trick is to override the sensation that you must be seen to be doing something to be effective, because doing nothing may be more appropriate.

Doing nothing is especially helpful when a pupil is reading and has come to a word they do not recognise. Most pupils will have been taught a range of strategies to help, such as phonics skills, referring to a picture for a clue, re-reading the sentence or returning to the word having read further on for more information. Pupils need time to think which of these strategies to deploy. It is easy to jump in too soon by suggesting they deploy a strategy or specify one to use. 'Use your phonics' or 'sound it out' are common responses provided by adults when hearing pupils read. Most pupils are aware of these strategies and do not need to be reminded of them. However, they need time to think through which strategy best fits the problem they are presented with.

Here is an example of where saying nothing can prompt a pupil to complete the task by herself. The group are reading a book which has the word 'icicles':

1 *TA:*   What are icicles?
2 *Ginny:*   They're ice that . . . they're ice that, um, like (*moves hand down and up*)
3 (*five-second pause*)
4 *Ginny:*   Hang down.

It was probably very tempting for the TA to help Ginny with the words she needed to complete her sentence in line 2, but the TA said nothing for five seconds (try doing this – it feels like an age!). Ginny went on to complete the sentence for herself in line 4.

So how much time should we give for pupils to think? Research shows that between three and five seconds after asking a question is valuable. Also (as in the above example), three to five seconds after an answer has been given allows time for the child to add more information. These techniques have been shown to improve children's attention and motivation (Rowe, 1986).

Verbal prompts

A verbal prompt should be designed to get the pupil to think some more and/or provide reassurance. Useful verbal prompts include the following examples:

- 'You have a think about what to do next'.
- 'What do you think you could do?'
- 'What is your plan?'
- 'I'm not sure – can you remember what the teacher said?'
- 'So you are not sure about that word. How could you work it out?'

REFLECTION ACTIVITY

Do you use these types of prompts with pupils you work with?

As in the last example, it can be helpful to state the problem for the child first. You will note that the words 'you' and 'think' feature in many of our examples. The key thing about a prompt is that it gets pupils to think more deeply and purposefully about the strategies they have used before. Prompts do not give any information to the pupil that will help them. What this means in practice is asking questions that remind pupils of what they already know and can do, in terms of both knowledge and skills, and the strategies that can unlock knowledge and skills inside their heads. We refer to this as TAs helping pupils to know what to do when they do not know what to do. We know of schools that have developed a bank of 'knowing what to do when you do not know what to do' questions to which teachers, TAs and pupils can refer. For pupils, practising asking themselves these questions when they are stuck improves their metacognitive and self-scaffolding capabilities.

Here is an example of verbal prompting. The pupils are writing an opening paragraph for a story.

1 *Kate:* How d'you spell 'these'?
2 *TA:* How could you find out? What could you do?
3 *Kate:* Er, look around.
4 *TA:* Mmm. You've got your words on the wall, haven't you?

Avoiding telling Kate how to spell 'these', the TA provides a prompt in line 2, followed by a second prompt. Kate comes up with a suitable strategy in line 3, which the TA acknowledges in line 4.

Prompts are particularly helpful for pupils who are able to carry out the task, but need some reassurance or someone to listen to their ideas. In this sense, prompts can be used as part of a wider strategy to build self-confidence.

Gesture

A non-verbal gesture, such as pointing to a prompt sheet, can encourage pupils to self-scaffold. It both reminds them of the process they need to follow and makes it more likely that they will go straight to the prompt sheet next time they are stuck. A common example is where children have difficulty in finding the right word; they may use the incorrect word or be searching for the correct one (this stalling is often accompanied by the child saying 'ahhh' or 'uhhh'). You can help by asking them to choose a self-help strategy from a prompt sheet. In the example below, the TA asks Kim about a picture of a trip to see Father Christmas.

1   *TA:*   And then what was this one?
2   *Kim:*   We went to uhhh *(five-second pause)*
3   *TA:*   *(points at prompt sheet)*
4   *Kim:*   *(picks up a pen and draws Santa)* Santa
5   *TA:*   Yes, we went to see Santa.

When Kim is unable to find the word (shown by 'uhhh'), the TA allows her some important thinking time. However, this is not enough for her to find the word that she is looking for. So next the TA next prompts her, through gesture, to look at her self-help sheet. This sheet is tailored to Kim's needs by suggesting three self-help strategies that she could use to find the word. Her options are to draw a picture, think of the first sound or think of something that rhymes with the word. She decides to draw a picture and this is sufficient for her to find the word without a model from the TA.

Gesture used in this way is the best strategy after silence. It should be used before pointing at a picture (which gives a clue), giving the first sound of the word (also a clue) or telling her the word (giving her a model). We describe clueing and modelling in more detail below.

Clueing

If a pupil you are supporting has been unable to self-scaffold, and the prompts you have given have not helped, you can move to the third layer of the scaffolding framework: clueing.

A clue gives the pupil a piece of information – or a hint – that will help them to work out what to do. It is, if you like, a heavier nudge than that provided by a prompt. In our research, we have found that TAs tend to give a clue too quickly; that is, they skip the prompting stage and instead provide too big a clue that gives away the answer. We suggest always starting with a small clue and adding additional clues, if needed. You can always supply a greater level of scaffolding, but if you give too much help straight away, you cannot undo the effects.

A good way to word a clue is as a question, the answer to which contains a key piece of information that will help the pupil. Here is an example in which a group is working on common digraphs (a single sound made up of two letters when written). The digraph that has been asked for is 'sh', and Nicole is having problems writing it.

1   *Nicole:*   *(sighs)*
2   *TA:*   Come on, Nicole. You remember sh.
3   *Nicole:*   I remember, but
4   *TA:*   Shhhop. What comes first? Two letters.
5   *Nicole:*   S H
6   *TA:*   Well done, sh.

In line 2, the TA provides a clue, as she knows that Nicole has done this recently ('You remember sh'). Further clues are provided in line 4. A word is given that contains the sound the group has used before, with an emphasis on the digraph needed ('shhhop'). This is then followed by a further clue ('Two letters'), which may or may not have been needed; we will never know. This is why providing only one clue at a time is important.

Clueing is trickier than prompting, as it is more reactive. Providing clues requires making fairly quick decisions about interactions in the moment. A common set of prompts can be developed over time, which can be applied in a range of situations, irrespective of which subject or task it relates to. As clues are specific to the task, the clues you provide will depend on which part the pupil is finding difficult and the level of their knowledge and understanding about the task. Being adequately informed about these things helps your decision-making and increases the appropriateness of the clues you provide. As we said in Chapter 3, being in the whole-class part of a lesson, when the teacher is explaining the task, is an important part of this.

Let's take another example, this time from a maths lesson. The TA is working with a group of 5- and 6-year-olds, and they are about to play a game in which they have to find the odd and even numbers. The group is having problems giving examples of odd and even numbers; they are giving a mix of correct and incorrect examples. The TA is responding to Colin, who has just given an incorrect even number. The answer the TA is looking for is the number two.

1	*TA:*	If you think above Miss Evans's desk, Colin, yeah, can you remember what we have above it?
2	*Colin:*	Oh yeah.
3	*TA:*	Miss Evans, where she sits, where Miss Evans sits.
4	*Colin:*	Seven.
5	*TA:*	What do we have? A road with houses, don't we? What do we call that?
6	*Colin:*	Er
7	*All:*	(*put hands up*)
8	*TA:*	Miss Evans calls it something. Can you remember?
9	*Colin:*	Odd and even street.
10	*TA:*	Yeah, odd and even street. And there are numbers at the top and numbers at the bottom. So let's think about the houses. I'm going to draw little houses here. OK.
11		At the top we're going to have our even numbers. Can you think what our even numbers are, Colin?
12	*Colin:*	Two.

In line 1, the TA gives a clue by reminding Colin about an 'odds and evens' poster that is above the teacher's desk, back in the classroom (the group is in another room). You will notice that, rather than telling him about the poster, she phrases it as a question. This puts the responsibility on Colin to remember the details himself. Although Colin acknowledges that there is something above the desk, in line 2 ('Oh yeah'), this does not move the interaction on. The TA, therefore, does not provide another clue in line 3, but just repeats information already available ('where Miss Evans sits'). This makes clear to Colin that he needs to provide more information. However, rather than giving more information about the poster, he provides another incorrect even number in line 4 ('seven'). Rather than focusing on this response, the TA provides an additional clue related to the poster ('A road with houses, don't we? What do we call that?'). This provides a further clue designed to connect the importance of recalling the details of the poster to the immediate task. Although all the pupils put their hands up in line 7, the TA perseveres with Colin, rephrasing the clue question in line 8. At no point is she tempted to provide the answer. Colin does name the poster correctly in line 9, and following the modelling of the poster in lines 10 and 11, he is able to name the first even number ('Two'). Through the use of clues, the odds and evens poster has now been established by the TA as a helpful resource for Colin to draw on.

Clueing is more difficult to provide than prompting. Prompts are at a general level and designed to remind pupils that they need to deploy acquired strategies, skills and knowledge in a variety of settings. Prompts can be developed and stored in your mind over time. Clues, however, are specific to the task being done. It will depend on which part the pupil is finding difficult and what their knowledge and understanding is about the task. So your clues are designed to provoke the pupil into drawing on a particular strategy, skill or piece of knowledge, which you know that they know of, or have some familiarity with. You need to know these things in order to make an informed and precise decision about the clue you are going to give.

REFLECTION ACTIVITY

Next time you are working with an individual or group for an extended period, try giving a prompt before a clue.

What language did you use? What effect did this have on the child?

Modelling

If your prompts and clues have not been successful in helping a pupil to move on, you will need to model part of the task. Modelling is the fourth tier of the interaction framework. A model demonstrates how to do the part of the task the pupil is unable to do. There are different ways of modelling, but they all involve showing the pupil what to do in easily replicable steps.

Providing a commentary

One way of modelling is to demonstrate how to do the part of the task that the pupil is finding difficult and provide a simultaneous commentary. The pupil can then 'replay the script' like a tape recording, out loud or in their head, as they repeat the steps you have modelled. Talking through this process aloud in the first person is particularly useful because using 'I' rather than 'you' helps to embed the steps in the pupil's mind as they replay your voice.

Here is an example of the commentary technique taken from a key stage 1 maths lesson:

1   *TA:*   So I'm going to have a turn. It [*the question*] says, How many? I'm going to count slowly, and I'm going to make sure that I mark every one off when I do it. So (*crossing off snowman each time*) 1, 2, 3, 4, 5, 6, 7, 8, 9. OK, I'm going to write 9 in the box.

As you can see, the TA has provided the pupil with a short script they can replay in order to carry out this particular part of the task. Ensuring the script is short and contains only a few steps aids recall. If there are too many steps, the pupil is likely to forget or get confused, and once again look to you for help. Each step provides a marker or reminder of the key action (italicised below) to take at each step:

'*How many* snowmen are there? . . . I'm going to *count slowly* . . . I'm going to *mark every one off* . . . I'm going to *write in the box* . . . '

This process supports the development of metacognition strategies, as it provides the pupil with a mental rehearsal. Ensuring that your commentary of instructions is delivered in the first person reduces the pupil's cognitive load; that is, they do not have to swap the 'you' for 'I' as they 'replay the tape'. In addition, the use of 'I' will help reinforce the pupil's ownership of the task.

REFLECTION ACTIVITY

Over the course of a day, note examples of your commentaries for pupils. Pay attention to your use of 'I' and 'you'.

Recasting

When you are modelling, there are occasions when it is more appropriate to use 'you' instead of 'I'. For example, when working on speech and language with children, we often need to 'recast' what they say. Recasting is repeating or reflecting a pupil's words, but in the correct form. For example:

1   *TA:*   What did you do at the weekend?
2   *Sam:*   I went Romford.
3   *TA:*   Oh, you went to Romford? That's interesting. What did you do there?

In this example, the incorrect sentence formation ('went Romford') has been recast by the TA in its correct form ('went to Romford'). The TA did this in such a way that it did not break up the flow of the interaction or draw attention to the error in a way that might damage Sam's confidence.

The golden rules of modelling

In summary, anything that gives pupils the opportunity to watch and listen to you do something correctly is called modelling. We do this when it is clear that the pupil is unable to achieve a particular process success criterion and our prompts and clues have not been successful. A good analogy for modelling is learning words in a new language. Languages are full of inconsistencies when it comes to how words are written and pronounced. Take, for example, the silent letters at the start of 'knight', at the end of 'hymn' and 'ballet', or in the middle of 'aisle' and 'plumber'. If we were learning English, our attempts to say these words would lead to understandable errors. In some cases, it is unlikely that prompting or clueing us towards the answer would work, as our prior knowledge on this particular issue is likely to be quite thin. So having our non-judgmental 'expert other' model by explaining the silent letter rule and sounding out new words will help us to learn. But we need to help ourselves by listening actively. This helps ensure that these new words and rules become embedded in our minds and increases our capacity to self-scaffold in the future.

Models are very important for learning. We all observe and listen to each other in order to learn how to do new things. We need to be clear, however, that when you are modelling in the classroom, it does not turn into a situation where you are doing the work, not the pupil! If not used carefully, modelling can have the opposite effect of what we are seeking to achieve: creating an over-dependence on adult help, rather than greater pupil independence.

These are our golden rules of modelling:

- Use modelling techniques if you are sure that the task is something the pupil cannot attempt by themselves with prompting or clueing.
- Modelling can also be used in situations when the pupil has done or said something incorrectly and it appears they are unaware of their error.
- Short, clear models work best, as they are more easily retained.
- Pupils must be actively listening. Some might need a cue to ensure they are attentive: 'I am going to model this step for you. I want you to look and listen carefully so you can try it by yourself when I finish'.
- Pupils needs to try it themselves as soon as possible after you have modelled. Make sure you encourage them to give it a go.

Correcting

Correcting is the last layer of our framework. Correcting is simply giving the pupil the answer or telling them how to do something. As will be clear by now, we advise steering clear of supplying pupils with answers.

Look at the following example. The group is reading words and then splitting them into the prefix and suffix. Ben is reading the word 'mistrust'.

1   *Ben:*   mmm mistrus
2   *TA:*   mistrust. So break it, make it mis and trust.

You can see that the TA not only corrects Ben's attempt to read the word (changing 'mistrus' to 'mistrust') but she also completes the task of identifying the prefix and suffix for him. The TA leapt to correction without applying techniques relating to the prior stages of our interaction framework. This example shows a TA giving a pupil the *most* amount of help first, when it is the least amount she should be aiming for.

REFLECTION ACTIVITY

What do you think are the key differences between modelling and correcting?

As we described above, modelling engages the pupil in the learning process through active listening and encourages them to replicate a set of clearly defined steps. This purposeful 'demonstration for learning' is absent from correcting.

To use our earlier analogy about learning words in a new language, you can imagine that having somebody correct your pronunciation each time you pronounced the silent 'k' at the start of words like 'knee', 'knot', know' and 'knit', without explaining that you are making an honest error, might become annoying and undermine your confidence. Alternatively, you might be quite happy to have someone correct you each time you make a mistake because it saves you the bother of doing it yourself!

Studying your interactions

In the schools we have worked in, TAs have learned a considerable amount about their practice by studying their own interactions. Often, they have done this in a group, which means they are able to support and learn from one another. This process has been invaluable for improving the quality of their interactions with pupils. We have applied some of these principles and ideas to a process you can try yourself. This can be easily adapted should you and other TAs in your school wish to collaborate.

Start by observing the teacher the next time you are in a whole-class session. Note down examples of the strategies they use, using the framework headings in the box below. Try to write down exactly what the teacher says.

Prompting

Clueing

Modelling

Correcting

To find out the frequency with which we use different types of interaction strategy, we need to pay attention to what we say and do when we are working with pupils. It is important to do this, as we can all fall into habits (which we may not be aware of) that have unintended outcomes in relation to developing pupil independence. So being reflective is an essential part of our professional development, and we should welcome and make time for studying what we do and how we can improve.

The very best way to study our interactions is to record them. This can be useful in helping us to see where we are 'over-supporting' pupils; that is, doing more for them than we need to. We have found that video recording is better than audio recording as it also lets us look at gestures, which are often used as part of clueing. Small portable video cameras are best for this exercise, and we have found the sound on these to be surprisingly good. Audio recording can also be helpful and may be more practical in some circumstances. Although the TAs we have worked with have often worried that the pupils will be distracted by the presence of a camera, they have been surprised at how quickly they get used to it and forget it is there. It is often the TA who takes longer to get used to it! So for all the activities in this section, you might find it helpful to record the session (audio or video) and play it back, or to pair up with another TA to observe each other.

REFLECTION ACTIVITY

When you next work with pupils, keep a simple tally chart of each time you use one of the strategies from the framework. We have not included self-scaffolding as this is something that the pupils will be doing rather than you. But we have included a row in which you can tally instances of waiting time, in which you can see if the pupil self-scaffolds. Limit your tallying time to no more than about ten minutes.

Strategy	Tally	Total instances
Silence/wait-time		
Prompting		
Clueing		
Modelling		
Correcting		

Look at the results on your tally chart. Note down anything that interests or surprises you.

You may want to repeat this exercise across a number of sessions to see if there are patterns in the ways you interact with pupils. For instance, do you tend to use a lot of clues, but fewer prompts?

Carry out the tally exercise again, but actively try to increase the use of strategies at the top of the triangle (particularly prompting) and decrease the ones at the bottom (particularly correcting).

Strategy	Tally	Total instances
Silence/wait-time		
Prompting		
Clueing		
Modelling		
Correcting		

Look at the results on your tally chart and compare them to your previous effort(s). Note down any similarities and differences.

You will find it very helpful to discuss your examples with other TAs and teachers. If you have a video, watching it with colleagues to identify examples and discuss practice is a great idea. Many schools we have worked with have used this as the basis for TA training and find it a very powerful form of professional development. In some schools, this process forms part of TAs' performance review. For example, in one school, TAs choose a short extract (up to ten minutes) as the basis of shared viewing and discussion.

Let's look at a transcript in detail to give you some practice in using the scaffolding framework. In the following example, the TA is working on a handwriting task with Tim. He is writing words which have the letter 'p' in them. The way that they have talked about letter formation previously is whether each part of the letter is in the grass, underground or in the sky.

What examples of wait-time, self-scaffolding, prompting, clueing, modelling and correcting can you find? Note that there may be more than one used in the same line. Mark them on the transcript itself or use the empty column on the right.

(continued)

(continued)

1	TA:	*(pointing at whiteboard)* Can you see where the head of the p sits?
2	Tim:	*(nods head)*
3	TA:	Where does he sit?
4	Tim:	*(points at p)*
5		*(three-second pause)*
6	Tim:	On the grass.
7	TA:	In the grass, OK. So.
8	Tim:	And mine's in the sky
9	TA:	Yeah, he's got his head in the sky, hasn't he? So if he's got his head
10		in the sky that means he's a capital p. And we don't want capital
11		p's because this p is at the end of lip. OK? So please try that one
12		again. *(starts to talk to another child)* How are we getting on? Oh,
13		they're beautiful. Well done.
14	Tim:	Shall I put it here?
15	TA:	What? Oh yeah. So if you stop. Oh yeah, they are tricky
16		ones. I'm going to do another one, just watch. So we're going
17		down, my tail's going into the ground. So it's descending, and then,
18		so the whole of the head of the p is in the grass.

Overall, how independent is this pupil being in this interaction?

Are there any parts where you would have done or said something different? Why?

You can read our ideas about this transcript in Appendix 3.

A summary of how to study your interactions

- Film a session where you are working with a pupil or group (or make an audio recording).
- Choose a section of the film/recording where the adult–pupil interactions interest you.
- Share the recording with at least one other TA, a teacher or the SENCO.
- Use the scaffolding framework to discuss the interaction.
- Discuss what you are doing to develop pupil independence.
- Identify one or two areas of your practice that you can develop.

Summary

In this chapter, we have discussed each part of the scaffolding framework in detail. We have clarified the rationale for the differences between the layers of the framework and the order in which they appear. We have set out strategies for you to try and provided 'real-world' examples to illustrate particular techniques. We have also set out a process for recording and reflecting on your own interactions, which we have used successfully with TAs.

A final note

Our work with schools has shown that the most powerful way to use this framework is at the whole-school level; that is, to adopt an approach to structuring effective interactions in classrooms that is used by all teachers, TAs and pupils, and shared with parents. We know from our research that there are a number of things that school leaders need to do in order to make this a reality, but do not lose sight of the fact that the greatest impact you can have on developing pupils' independent learning and decision-making can be derived from using the framework to inform the strategies you use in moment-by-moment interactions.

We have said already that, when it comes to witnessing and influencing learning, TAs have a ringside seat. Throughout this chapter, we have emphasised how you need to use scaffolding strategies as you work with pupils. But as well as interacting with pupils to ensure they remain in charge of their own learning journey, you are also in a position to add considerable value to what teachers do, by capturing the detail of those journeys. In the next chapter, we will explore how you can provide valuable feedback for teachers on pupils' learning, effort and engagement, which is essential for good assessment and planning.

References

Giangreco, M. F. (2010) One-to-one paraprofessionals for students with disabilities in inclusive classrooms: Is conventional wisdom wrong? *Intellectual and Developmental Disabilities*, 48, pp. 1–13. Available online at: www.uvm.edu/~cdci/archives/mgiangre/IDD2010%2048(1)%201-13.pdf (accessed 17 April 2015).

Rowe, M. B. (1986) Wait-time: Slowing down may be a way of speeding up. *Journal of Teacher Education*, 37, pp. 43–50.

Further reading

Radford, J., Blatchford, P. and Webster, R. (2011) Opening up and closing down: Comparing teacher and TA talk in mathematics lessons. *Learning and Instruction*, 21(5), pp. 625–635.

Radford, J., Bosanquet, P., Webster, R. and Blatchford. P. (2015) Scaffolding learning for independence: Clarifying teacher and TA roles for children with SEN. *Learning and Instruction*, 36, pp. 1–10.

Radford, J., Bosanquet, P., Webster, R., Blatchford, P. and Rubie-Davies. C. (2014) Fostering learner independence through heuristic scaffolding: A valuable role for teaching assistants. *International Journal of Educational Research*, 63(1), pp. 116–126.

Chapter 5

Assessment for learning

Providing valuable feedback for teachers and pupils

Throughout this book, we have highlighted the privileged position that TAs have within the classroom: you are present at the moment learning happens. That said, learning is not something we can see directly, but we *can* observe its effects in the form of pupils' performances; that is, in the things they say and the work they produce. It is this detailed information on pupil performance that teachers need in order to inform their planning and teaching. Put another way, quality feedback helps teachers to do their job more effectively, and the more rich and informed the feedback is, the better the teaching. And of course, when teaching improves, so does pupil performance.

In this chapter, we will look at your role in providing the valuable feedback that is the fuel for better teaching. Building on the previous chapter, we also consider how to provide feedback for pupils and how to support their own assessment of their performance.

As we have consistently argued, it is the teacher who has overall responsibility for planning work for all the pupils in the class. By keeping clear records, you can provide valuable information for teachers about the performance of pupils you work with. The type of feedback teachers need in order to inform good assessment relate to: 1) the level of independence with which each pupil has achieved the process success criteria; and 2) the type and amount of scaffolding each pupil needed, if any. And of course, this information is best recorded in the moment, as you work with pupils.

Although we are not suggesting that TAs take on pupil assessment in any significant measure (because that remains the responsibility of teachers), it is important to understand the difference between assessment *of* learning and assessment *for* learning. This is because the forms of feedback that serve each type of assessment are quite different.

REFLECTION ACTIVITY

*Use the table below to list the features of assessment **of** learning and assessment **for** learning. Compare the lists. What do you notice?*

Assessment of learning	Assessment for learning

Assessment of learning

Your lists may have contained the words 'tests' or 'exams'. These terms might naturally spring to mind because they are such significant features of our education system. Tests and examinations are examples of assessment *of* learning, or 'summative assessment'. Summative assessment is a summary of what a pupil knows and what they can do, at the point in time the test was taken. This type of assessment is often used at the end of a school year or key stage; for example, SATs at the end of key stage 2 and GCSEs taken by 16-year-olds.

Teachers also produce assessments of learning in the shape of end-of-year reports. These reports summarise the knowledge, skills and competencies pupils have developed over the school year. To compile a report, a teacher draws not just on test results, but on information they have observed and recorded over the year on the pupil's performance: marks in their exercise books; observations of them at work; conversations with them; and, very often, feedback from TAs.

Diagnostic tests are also examples of assessment of learning. These are tests that check where a pupil is in relation to a very specific set of developmental skills. Diagnostic tests are often used when there are concerns about a child's development and may be used to determine the extent to which they have a specific learning need or developmental delay. An example would be a phonics check in literacy. The pupil would be asked to read aloud a list of words containing the key phonemes they are expected to know by a particular point in time. Alternatively, the phonemes might be read aloud and the pupil is asked to write them down. In maths, a pupil might be tested on their knowledge of place value and basic number operations (addition, subtraction, multiplication and division), with the questions read out to the pupil. Such tests help teachers and SEN professionals isolate and identify pupils' difficulties with understanding.

REFLECTION ACTIVITY

> *List examples of assessment **of** learning activities used in your school.*

Assessments of learning help practitioners pinpoint where a pupil is developmentally, in relation to where they are expected to be for their age. These forms of testing help schools identify pupils that are falling behind in various respects. However, assessment of where a pupil is developmentally (relative to their age or peer group) does not in itself produce information that can support future learning. These are useful tools for informing us of what a child can do *now*, but they are unable to tell us what the child needs to do *next*, and how to help them achieve this. Nor are these assessments very helpful in determining the extent to which a child is able to work independently. To obtain this information, we need to look to the methods of assessment *for* learning.

Assessment for learning

The term assessment *for* learning, or 'formative assessment', concerns the actions we take to change the way we work with a pupil. Having used summative assessment methods to determine what a pupil can do at a specific point in time, we use this information to maximise their future learning experiences. This might require planning a new task or making adaptations to an existing task, or it might be that we need to provide constructive feedback to help the pupil move on. It can also take the form of providing scaffolding around a particular skill. However good the assessment *of* pupil progress is at the end of a task, it remains assessment *of* learning *until* that information is used in the planning process. When this information is used to modify and individualise a pupil's learning experiences, it becomes assessment *for* learning, and therefore much more valuable to the pupil in terms of enhancing their learning journey. Assessment for learning is often described as a cycle, as shown in Figure 5.1.

You can see that planning is based on the pupil's progress, which is then benchmarked against the process success criteria of the task. This information is used to plan the next step in the pupil's development and, in turn, leads to the development of new or modified tasks and new process success criteria. The new criteria might mirror or overlap with those relating to the previous task, as the pupil might need to practise them in order to grow their confidence and their ability to perform the task

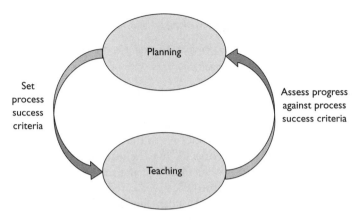

Figure 5.1 The assessment for learning cycle

with increasing independence. Some might be new process success criteria that build on things they have proven they can already do independently. You can see that a thorough understanding of child development and relevant subject knowledge are essential for effective task planning and teaching.

The leading researchers in assessment for learning are Paul Black and Dylan Wiliam. Their most widely discussed paper is called *Inside the Black Box*, published in 1998. In it, they argue that learning is interactive and that the teacher needs to adapt the learning experience for the pupil so it matches their specific needs. This is one of the key principles on which we have based this book. Black and Wiliam say that the information collected on pupils' performance, as an indicator of their learning, is essential to achieving this match. They also put a value on the assessments pupils carry out on their own work. We will discuss pupil self-assessment later in this chapter.

Quality feedback: the role of the TA in the assessment for learning cycle

We know that the core components of summative assessment (assessment *of* learning) help the teacher to decide the appropriate next steps and level of support for each pupil (assessment *for* learning). Without this vital information, the teacher has only the product of the task (e.g. a piece of writing), produced by the pupil, to help them make constructive decisions about what further tasks are required to advance their learning and develop their independence. This information, as we discussed in Chapter 3 using our cheese sandwich exercise, is a much less reliable indicator of what a pupil can do independently. In this section, we look at an effective way of providing quality feedback on pupil performance for teachers.

REFLECTION ACTIVITY

Think about your current experience regarding feedback to teachers and answer the following questions:

Do teachers ask you for feedback on pupils' performance?

What information, if any, do you collect on pupils' performance?

In the main, do you record this information as they are working or after lessons?

How specific is the information you record? Do you consider, for example, the nature and amount of the support needed or given (e.g. prompts, clues, models)?

How do you give feedback to teachers you work with? Is it mainly verbally or in writing?

As well as having those vital moment-by-moment interactions with pupils, TAs can perform a valuable role in capturing pupils' responses to their efforts and the teacher-set tasks in the form of providing 'live feedback'. It is helpful to walk through an example of what we mean by providing 'live feedback'. Take this science task from a key stage 3 lesson, where the overall goal of the task was to predict the outcomes of an experiment: what happens to different materials when they are placed in water. The process success criteria were:

- Say what I think will happen.
- Give at least one reason why I think this.
- Give relevant evidence to support my prediction.

The TA working with a group of four pupils kept the following record, benchmarking their progress against the process success criteria. She observed the pupils working and logged the following information:

	Name			
Process success criteria	Ragu	Samina	Lesley	Rizwan
Say what I think will happen, e.g. I think the lithium will fizz.	✓	✓	✓	P
Give at least one reason why I think this, e.g. It reacts with water.	P	P	✓	P
Give relevant evidence to support the prediction, e.g. It is close to potassium in the periodic table.	C	M	C	M

Key:

✓   Can do this independently
P   Can do with prompting
C   Can do with clues
M   Modelled for the child

There was also space on the feedback sheet to add useful notes for the teacher on specific difficulties, how resources were used or helpful prompts. The TA in the science lesson made the following notes alongside her observations:

I had to introduce the idea of the periodic table. Ragu and Lesley helped find lithium on the periodic table and were able to remember what happened to the potassium last week and, with clues, made the link.

Early years practitioners are familiar with making observations and taking notes as pupils work, but this practice seems to disappear further up the schooling system. This is a shame, as direct observation and on-the-spot record-keeping is a reliable way of providing accurate information about what pupils can do and what they find difficult. If you make notes after the event, you run the risk of your recollections being unreliable or missing things out. Consistent with the SEN Code of Practice, this type of record-keeping is particularly essential for pupils with learning needs or who have difficulty carrying out the tasks set by the teacher. Your role as the TA is highly valuable, as you are present at the moments of success and struggle, and have the opportunity to record in detail how pupils manage their own learning, what you did to help, at which points (and in what ways) you made your intervention and how they responded. This information also provides the basis for dialogue with pupils about their learning as they work.

Using the information recorded by the TA and each pupil's assessment of their own work, the science teacher planned a similar task for the next lesson, adding notes to the lesson plan for the TA about the resources or adaptations which might be needed:

Potential difficulty	Resource/adaptation
Giving evidence to support the prediction,	Use the key questions about the materials involved when making predictions,
e.g. Where it is in the periodic table and how this relates to the material's properties.	e.g. What are the properties of this material? Where is the material in the periodic table? What other materials are near it and share similar properties? Encourage them to use the facts about materials when giving reasons.

As we have already suggested, you can never be sure in advance exactly which parts of a task a pupil might find easy or challenging. But the assessment for learning cycle means that the teacher can use what they know about the pupil (what they know/do not know and what they can/cannot do) to set a task that offers the appropriate level of challenge. Furthermore, the teacher can think about how the pupil might be helped to access the parts of the task they are likely to find difficult.

The recording format we have suggested makes it easy for a teacher to see at a glance whether the task has been pitched at the correct level for each pupil. This feedback then informs the teacher's decisions about how to adapt the planning for next time. Teachers will find this rich information invaluable and should plan this into the role they ask you to take in lessons.

REFLECTION ACTIVITY

What would the following feedback tell the teacher about the task that they had planned? Note: it is the TAs' coding under each pupil's name that is important here, not the specific process success criteria (which we have left blank).

Process success criteria	Name			
	Ragu	Samina	Lesley	Rizwan
1	✓	✓	✓	✓
2	✓	✓	✓	✓
3	✓	✓	✓	P

✓   Can do this independently
P   Can do with prompting
C   Can do with clues
M   Modelled for the child

As you will no doubt have concluded, the teacher, presented with a feedback form almost full of ticks, is likely to arrive at the view that the task was well within the pupils' ability to complete. They would know that the pupils in the group could be given a more challenging task next time. They might also question why they allocated a TA to work with this group, as they were (with one exception) able to complete each part of the task independently.

The allocation of TA support should be carefully considered, and TAs should be deployed by the teacher to work with a group that is likely to benefit from their specific expertise in scaffolding. However, as we noted earlier, the teacher cannot be sure how challenging pupils will find any given task. So, in this instance, all is not lost, as the TA has provided a useful service in collecting valuable data on the pupils' learning journey.

REFLECTION ACTIVITY

What would the feedback below tell the teacher about the task that they had planned? Again, it is not the specifics of the particular process success criteria that are relevant.

Process success criteria	Name			
	Ragu	Samina	Lesley	Rizwan
1	C	C	M	C
2	M	M	M	M
3	M	C	M	M

✓   Can do this independently
P   Can do with prompting
C   Can do with clues
M   Modelled for the child

A teacher receiving this helpful feedback would conclude that the task was perhaps too challenging for these pupils. The records provided by the TA show that the pupils required high levels of support for all of the process success criteria, mainly in the form of models or clues. The reflective teacher would realise that, in the next lesson, these pupils would need further opportunities to practise criterion 1. The teacher would also need to think through alternatives to criteria 1 and 2, and perhaps break these 'mini-goals' down further. The group may need to be given an opportunity to consolidate an earlier concept or skill, or to do (or redo) a similar task. Again, adult support would be available to scaffold as necessary, and the TA would record the level of independence the pupils demonstrated.

REFLECTION ACTIVITY

Trial using the feedback sheet with a teacher you work with. This can be found in Appendix 4 or downloaded from http://maximisingtas.co.uk.

After a few uses, review how it went? Is it useful? Could the feedback sheet be modified to better suit your needs?

How could the role of TAs in the assessment for learning cycle be improved in your school?

Feedback to pupils

Black and Wiliam (1998) concluded that formative feedback is a key part of assessment for learning. Formative feedback is also rated as one of the *most* effective ways of improving pupil progress.[1] It provides very specific information for the pupil on which parts of the task they have succeeded in and how to develop their understanding and skills relating to the parts not yet achieved. In this way, feedback becomes a positive process that focuses on moving learning forward. Crucially, this type of feedback reinforces the idea that it is the *learning* that is important, not the mark or grade given at the end. This principle underlies the ideas about developing a growth mindset that we discussed in Chapter 2.

REFLECTION ACTIVITY

Think about your current practice regarding giving feedback to pupils and answer the following questions:

When do you provide feedback to pupils? Do you do this while they are working or at the end of a task or lesson?

What type of information do you feed back to pupils?

To what extent is your feedback focused on the completion of the task?

To what extent is your feedback focused on pupils' progress towards process success criteria?

To what extent is your feedback focused on pupils' progression towards independent working?

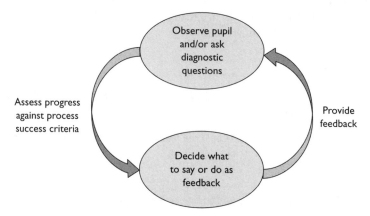

Figure 5.2 Contingent teaching cycle

Remember: each process success criteria is a mini-goal. The pupil will need to know the goal they are working on at each point in the activity, and have specific feedback on progress towards this goal *as they work*. We can think of this process, which is represented in Figure 5.2 above, as a smaller version of the assessment for learning cycle. This 'cycle within the cycle' links to the idea of contingent teaching, which we covered in Chapter 3.

Focusing on one process success criteria at a time can be helpful for pupils who feel overwhelmed by tasks, or find it difficult to get started. When the task has been split into 'chunks', the struggling pupil needs only to work on the first chunk. The first step is often the hardest for those that find it difficult to make a start, so the sense of achievement gained from completing the first of the process success criteria can provide positive momentum. Pupils will still need feedback even as they become more skilled at particular types of tasks. However, you need to fade support out over time, giving feedback less frequently in order to encourage pupils to work independently, and for increasingly longer periods of time.

At the lesson level, progress might be reviewed after a short period, which might be agreed with the pupil. For example, you might say: 'OK, how about you do the next two parts of the task and then check back with me? I think that will take you five minutes'. Then later, you might say: 'You seem to be fine with these now, so I would like you to carry on by yourself. How long do you think you need to complete the next two steps?' As a key part of the progression to independent working, pupils also need assistance to evaluate their own progress against goals. This is the focus of our final section.

Self-assessment

Pupils' ability to self-assess their performance is an essential component of Black and Wiliam's concept of assessment for learning. In order to develop independence, pupils need the language and tools to assess their own progress against the overall task goal. To do this, they need to be able to:

- identify the process success criteria (mini-goals) that comprise the task;
- have a clear idea of what success looks like for each of the process success criteria;
- check their progress against each criterion;
- plan a way to move from where they are to where they need to be.

The ability to do this is the basis for independent learning. This is a complex set of skills that can be difficult to acquire, but forms the basis of lifelong learning. Once we develop these capacities to a proficient level, we can apply them to more or less any problem we encounter. We can deploy the independent learning skills of planning, problem-solving and evaluating (see Chapter 2) to a wide range of challenges, and approach them with a sense of confidence. We can help pupils to acquire these essential skills by providing scaffolding in the same way that we would for any other skills. We have observed TAs doing this in a variety of ways. Here are some examples.

Identifying process success criteria:

- Encouraging pupils to make their own notes as the teacher explains or models.
- Encouraging pupils to identify the process success criteria, with the TA scribing.
- Pupils using notes made by the TA to develop process success criteria.

Identifying the attributes of success:

- Modelling a particular step in the process correctly and incorrectly, then asking pupils to highlight which is better and why.
- Using examples, discussing the features of an accomplished piece of work.
- Using examples, discussing the features of a less satisfactory piece of work, and encouraging pupils to identify where the work falls short and what could be improved.

Checking their progress against process success criteria:

- Ensuring process success criteria are clearly visible as pupils work and encouraging them to check their progress against each criterion. The frequency of reminders can be faded out over time.
- Ensuring the scaffolding framework is clearly visible as pupils work and encouraging them to work through the layers themselves. This will ensure that they have 'earned' the right for a clue or for something to be modelled.
- The TA and pupil sharing the completion of the feedback sheet (see Appendix 4).

Planning how to move from where pupils are to where they need to be:

- Discussing the process success criteria pupils need to practise and the level of support they feel they require. Remember: the least amount first!
- Helping pupils to make decisions about how and when they can practise the things they find challenging. For example, could they ask the teacher for some specific homework?

Common methods of self-assessment include 'two stars and a wish', which teachers often ask pupils to think about at the end of a lesson. Pupils write down two things they think is good about their work and one thing they think could be improved. It is also worth asking *how* pupils could achieve their wish. Another similar approach is 'what went well and even better if'.

Self-assessment can be tricky, and some pupils might lack the self-confidence required to do this. Others might have particular problems when thinking about their learning. These pupils will need help from you to scaffold their way through this task effectively. Providing a commentary or having dialogue with pupils about their learning, in the moment, can be powerful as it can make learning processes visible and therefore easier to access, modify and record. Capturing those moments of break-through that indicate learning can be powerful reminders to pupils that, yes, they *can* do it! These instances are the building blocks of a growth mindset (see Chapter 2).

It is vitally important that pupils are involved in the assessment of their own learning and that they have a clear sense of ownership over their learning. Some pupils may need support or encouragement to identify areas requiring additional practice, but the overarching aim is to ensure that pupils feel responsible for their own learning and are able to identify what they need to do in order to move their own learning along independently.

The benefits and implications of empowering pupils in this way should be self-evident, but one way in which it seems particularly relevant is in terms of giving pupils with SEN a voice in provision review processes, such as the Annual Review for pupils with an Education, Health and Care Plan (EHCP) or a Statement. Much like the effective interactions we have been describing in this book, the SEN Code of Practice makes it clear that the focus of EHCPs is on outcomes; that is, what we want the pupil to be able to do.

Outcomes are agreed by the school, parents/carers and sometimes other agencies (e.g. clinicians or the educational psychology service). The Code of Practice states that children and young people should also have a stake in the planning and reviewing progress. The more a pupil is able to take ownership for short term (e.g. lesson length) learning goals, the more likely it is that they will have the motivation, confidence and skills to take a full part in the process of reviewing and setting the medium and longer-term goals that affect their education.

REFLECTION ACTIVITY

Do pupils in your school assess their own learning? What strategies do they use?

What questions could you ask pupils to help them assess their own learning as they work.

Self-assessment

Reflect on what has been covered in this chapter. What elements of assessment for learning have you successfully put in place?

What areas could you improve on and how?

What would help you to achieve this?

Summary

In this chapter, we have laid out a role for TAs that is consistent with the process of assessment for learning. A significant part of this role is to collect accurate and detailed feedback *of* learning for the teacher to use in assessment *for* learning. This can then be used to inform the teacher's planning of the next task. We have described a way in which TAs can capture evidence of pupils' ability to accomplish mini-goals independently and the type of support needed to move them towards this. We covered the importance of feedback to pupils, which refers back to the ideas of contingent teaching from earlier in the book. Finally, we considered how TAs can support pupils' efforts to assess their own performance, as part of the wider drive to ensure they achieve independence. For children and young people, this is likely to extend to wider processes of review and target-setting. The role we have described for TAs within the assessment process underpins the broader aim of developing a growth mindset and pupils' capacity and confidence to take greater ownership over their learning.

Note

1 https://educationendowmentfoundation.org.uk/toolkit/toolkit-a-z/feedback/ and http://visible-learning.org/hattie-ranking-influences-effect-sizes-learning-achievement/

References

Black, P. and Wiliam, D. (1998) *Inside the black box: Raising standards through classroom assessment*. London: GL Assessment Limited.

Chapter 6

Promoting effective group work

The research evidence is clear that, compared with teachers, TAs spend much more time working with pupils in groups. Observations in primary schools conducted as part of the DISS project showed that TAs spent 41 per cent of their time working with small groups (groups of between two and five pupils) and 21 per cent working with medium-sized groups (six to ten pupils). The proportion of time TAs in secondary schools spent working with small and medium groups was 17 per cent and 1 per cent, respectively. Teachers in both settings, on the other hand, spent 8 per cent of their time working with (mainly small) groups (Blatchford, Russell and Webster, 2012). A similar situation was found in the Making a Statement study: observations in primary classrooms showed that TAs worked with small groups 50 per cent more often than teachers (Webster and Blatchford, 2013).

It is difficult to dispute that it is TAs, rather than teachers, that have the greater opportunity to have what we might call 'quality time' working with pupils in groups. It is vital, therefore, that we capitalise on this situation.

In this chapter, we build on the book's coverage so far by discussing how to support pupils in group settings. First, we look at the type of support required to help pupils ask one another for help and to provide help to others when working *in* groups. This will be familiar territory for many TAs. However, there is generally less information on how to support pupils when they work *as* groups; that is, how to support collaborative activities where there is a team goal. This is the focus of the second half of this chapter.

REFLECTION ACTIVITY

Do you have a different role when pupils work collaboratively as a group compared to when pupils work on individual tasks in groups?

Supporting pupils working *in* groups: pupil-to-pupil scaffolding

No doubt you often work with groups where each pupil has a different or differentiated task. The outcomes may differ, but the self-scaffolding and problem-solving strategies we discussed in Chapter 4 are still relevant here, and you should encourage pupils to use them. In particular, pupils should be encouraged to talk about their learning to a peer. Strangely, asking the others sitting with them is not something that often occurs to pupils. It may be because pupils have become used to having TAs close by and asking them when they hit a problem. Peer-to-peer support is a good failsafe for occasions when a TA or teacher is unavailable. In many ways, it has a power of its own in terms of improving pupils' conceptual understandings and social skills (Baines, Blatchford and Webster, 2015).

If we want pupils to be effective learners, we need to help them develop the skills of accessing peer support and allow opportunities for them to practise. We also need pupils to understand how to be a good supporter of learning, so that when a class-mate asks them for help, they give help constructively and avoid giving away the answer or doing the work for them.

Asking peers for support

It is important that pupils are aware that asking another member of the group for assistance is a legitimate form of support. It is a clear way in which pupils can be seen to take ownership of their learning. For some pupils, it might be necessary to break up the option of talking to a peer into smaller steps:

1   Choosing who to talk to.
2   Making a suitable approach.
3   Phrasing a specific question.

These things may be obvious to you as a skilled learner, but they can be less so to pupils with weak social skills and low self-confidence. These pupils will often have a negative perception of themselves as a learner; they are archetypal 'fixed mindsetters'. Exposing their weaknesses to others comes with a risk that tends not to trouble 'growth mindset-ters'. So even if they *know* asking a classmate is an option, it is a strategy some pupils are unlikely to deploy for fear of attracting ridicule, because to others it could look as if they do not understand. It is essential, then, that pupils are confident and comfort-able with asking others for help. Practice, together with support from you, will enable confidence to grow.

Let us explore the three steps above in detail, using the elements of the scaffolding framework to work through the type of support you can provide when pupils are working in groups. As we work through these steps, you might additionally consider how these strategies might be used in the wider setting of the whole class.

Step 1: choosing who to talk to

In the first instance, we want all pupils to manage their own learning. However, if a pupil does not use a self-scaffolding strategy when they are unsure how to proceed, they can be prompted to find one by using the 'knowing what to do when you do not know what to do' techniques we covered in Chapter 4 (perhaps subtly emphasising strategies that involve asking a peer). Yet, as we have mentioned already, there will be some pupils who need to build up to this step. Despite their best efforts, they may be unable to use a self-scaffolding strategy because their low self-confidence gets in the way, even in a small-group setting. They could become frozen when working through the finer points of making an approach or phrasing their question. In this situation, you need to ask some deliberate questions to help them overcome their anxieties. Here are some examples of clues you could use:

- Would talking to someone else help?
- Is there someone you feel comfortable talking to?
- Who on the table has already done that part of the task and might be able to help?

Pupils might need some assistance in terms of identifying the best person in the group to help them. They may be tempted to pick their friend, but this decision needs to be based on who is most likely to be the 'expert other' and the best source of help. Naturally, you are a viable option here, and it might be that in particular circumstances it is right that you provide the support. However, in the first instance, pupils should be encouraged to think carefully about which of the other group members has a particular aptitude for achieving a specific task or completing a process, and is able to share their techniques and tips. This may require further prompting. For example, when drawing a butterfly in an art activity, it can be tricky to achieve the mirror image of the wing shape and pattern. Therefore, the group's resident artist would be well placed to advise on how to achieve this, potentially in the style of formative feedback (see Chapter 5).

Step 2: making a suitable approach

Having identified an appropriate peer, the pupil will need to think about making a suitable approach. Something simple like 'Hi, can you help me with this?' is a good first approach. This is important, as some pupils (for various reasons) do not have a complete sense of how to initiate social interaction, so they need assistance to formulate a question and possibly an opportunity to practise asking it. Asking the pupil some particular questions about the purpose and wording of the approach may be required.

You may set in place some additional provisions to boost the confidence of pupils who are particularly anxious about approaching children in other groups in the wider classroom setting. For example, you could write the approach question out and allow the pupil to rehearse it with you before asking their classmate. This temporarily reduces the pupil's cognitive load, as not having to recall the wording of the question allows them to deal with the emotional elements of the task (e.g. building up courage and overcoming nerves).

You could secretly engineer the first few attempts so that the pupil who will be approached is aware that their classmate will ask them a question and that a friendly and helpful response is appreciated. The main emphasis here is in providing opportunities to help the anxious pupil overcome their fears about approaching and initiating interaction with others. If their initial experiences of asking others for help are positive, and their fears about rejection are not realised, vulnerable pupils will grow in confidence and, over time, use this technique for learning.

Step 3: phrasing a specific question

You can, if needed, use prompts and clues to help the pupil word the specific learning question that they have. You might also model what to say. We know from our research and work in schools that TAs are very good at doing this with teachers. TAs role-play how to ask for help in front of the whole class. TAs can, of course, model exactly the same process, but ask another child instead of the teacher. Following this idea, you might, for example, first identify the problem by saying: 'I'm not sure how to do this next bit. I'm going to ask Arthur for some help'. The next step is to model an approach and ask a specific question about the bit you are stuck with; for example: 'Excuse me, Arthur. I'm not sure what to do when I finish question 4. What did you do?'

Even though they know the answer, TAs model how to ask the type of questions one asks when stuck or uncertain. This has an added value in terms of not only demonstrating that it is OK not to know the answer, but also that it is perfectly acceptable, and indeed encouraged, to ask for help when you hit a problem with your learning that you are unable to overcome by yourself. What is more, doing this in front of the class or a group is likely to help others who are struggling on the same part of the task, but are perhaps too shy to ask for help in front of their peers. Over time, the mystique and stigma about admitting what pupils (and adults) do not know, and the value of bringing this out into the public space of the classroom, can create a fertile environment for learning and enquiry.

REFLECTION ACTIVITY

Observe the pupils you work with as they undertake a task.

How frequently do they talk to one another about learning? How often do they ask each other for help when they are unsure what to do?

Who does each pupil speak to? Do they have a 'favourite'?

How are interactions initiated and questions asked?

Are there any pupils who talk to their peers less than others when they are stuck? Why might this be?

What might help to encourage these pupils to interact with their peers in order to move their learning forward?

Providing support to peers

When working with a group, you will almost certainly have seen and heard pupils either giving someone else the answer (correcting) or, perhaps more significantly, ignoring or dismissing those who ask for help or who otherwise demonstrate a clear need for support. Baines *et al.* (2015) note that 'closing out' disadvantaged pupils is common in classrooms. Often this is because those in need of help have underdeveloped social and/or communication skills, so this inhibits interaction. Some children are shy, and their withdrawn behaviour can lead to them being shut out by others. Conversely, pupils can find it difficult to work with those with dominant or aggressive personalities or those with unusual mannerisms (e.g. being overfamiliar) because of the way their behaviour can disrupt the harmony of the group. As a consequence, these pupils do not always present themselves as able to provide support to others.

What is more, pupils who receive a high amount of TA support are not always obvious candidates to approach for support, as the class typically sees that these pupils need a lot of help themselves. Over time, this high-level support can inadvertently affect the general relationships TA-supported pupils have with other pupils. For example, as popularity tends to be based on opportunities to interact with other children without interference from adults, the development of friendship groups happens *away* from – and not including – supported pupils.

Some of the suggestions in the previous section are predicated on pupils knowing how to give useful support to others when working in groups. The need for *all* pupils to become skilled at this can be achieved by teaching them to use the scaffolding framework when they interact with one another. TAs' and teachers' efforts need to be particularly strong in helping less confident and vulnerable pupils to develop these skills.

REFLECTION ACTIVITY

Ask some pupils what they do when another pupil asks them how to do something.

What strategies do they use for helping others?

How do they know if others find these strategies helpful?

You can talk to pupils about the scaffolding framework and teach them to use it with each other in the ways we have outlined in this book. The key is to make sure pupils understand the principle of giving the least amount of help first. In many cases, the pupil that is approached for help will not be aware of what the other pupil has done to help themselves, as she would have been busy on her own task. Therefore, you can explore what types of questions and statements would be appropriate and helpful to ask in such a situation. Here are some examples:

- What methods have you tried so far?
- I will explain which methods I have tried, so you can see if any might help.
- Have you gone back through each step to work out where you have gone wrong?
- Work through each step again with me. I will try to identify where you might have gone wrong.
- Would you like some feedback on your work? I might be able to suggest where you could improve. You could do the same for me.

In Chapter 2, we explained the significance of ensuring that pupils see the purpose in a particular piece of learning and making it relevant to the 'real world'. Having conversations about how the scaffolding framework can aid learning and improve performance should be a relatively easy sell, as the aim is to give pupils more options and techniques to self-scaffold. It also gives them a suite of tools to assist others and so opens up opportunities for social interaction and the development of positive peer relations.

For the youngest children, an effective way of talking about the framework is to use a puppet to help them practise scaffolding another pupil's learning. Starting with a task you know the child can do, or a concept they understand, you can encourage them to talk to the puppet (voiced by you) through a particular problem it is stuck with. The child can then practise:

- asking the puppet if it has had a good think (and other prompts);
- giving clues: starting with small clues and working up to bigger clues if the puppet is still stuck;
- modelling: showing the puppet how to do something.

You can adjust how much support the child should give depending on which of these skills you want them to practise.

Older pupils need time and opportunities to practise these things too. In our experience, pupils respond well to having the scaffolding framework available (on a laminated card or on a classroom display) and being allowed to reflect at the end of a session on how they used it to support others. We have included a copy in Appendix 5 for this purpose. The type of questions they should consider include:

- Has anybody asked you for help with the task?
- What level of scaffolding did you use to help them?
- Can you give an example of what you said to them?
- Did the wording of the question/request for help affect the amount of support you gave?
- Did your scaffolding help? If so, how? If not, why do you think it was unsuccessful?

It is important that all pupils feel they are able to both ask for support and provide it to others, not only when they work in groups, but in other settings too. It is essential that pupils develop the self-confidence and the tools to ask peers for help, especially those who are at risk of becoming dependent on adult support. The effects of being able to ask for help and give help can be liberating for pupils, and it has the potential to reshape the learning culture of the classroom. You can facilitate this process by helping pupils to redirect queries to other pupils who you know can help, and to help them develop expertise in providing support to others.

REFLECTION ACTIVITY

Put into practice the ideas about how to support pupils in group settings regarding asking for help and providing help. Try the two reflection activities on pages 91 and 92 again and use your notes to create a 'before and after' picture. Compare the two sets of findings. What do you notice?

Supporting pupils working *as* groups: collaborative learning

The principles of effective group work

In this section, we draw on techniques that emerged from the SPRinG project, led by Peter Kutnick and Peter Blatchford. SPRinG, which stands for Social Pedagogic Research into Group Work, investigated how teachers can make better use of groups as a vehicle for learning. The techniques, co-developed with teachers, form part of a structured approach to developing the reciprocal scaffolding skills pupils need to complete activities while working *as* a group. We have also drawn on Neil Mercer's idea of 'exploratory talk' (1995), which is useful for enhancing pupils' experiences of collaborative work.

The SPRinG approach to group work is based on a set of principles that fall within the jurisdiction of teachers. These include: effective classroom management and grouping arrangements (e.g. seating plans), good group composition (e.g. which pupils and how many) and appropriate task setting. As with all other tasks, the expectation is that the teacher designs the collaborative activity for the group.

Many tasks that claim to be collaborative do not, in fact, *require* pupils to work together. A board game, for example, is not truly collaborative, even if it does promote group interaction. A collaborative task must *require all* group members to participate and contribute to a group goal. In order to achieve the goal, pupils need to be able to work together as a team. Perhaps not surprisingly, this is easier to achieve in smaller groups because tasks can be more carefully designed to push learning to the next level of development.

'Jigsawing', for example, is a useful task technique that allows pupils to work as a group to research information on a particular topic (for example, aspects of life in ancient Egypt or the properties of different types of plastic). The groups are then mixed up, so that in each one there is an 'expert' from each of the original groups who shares the information their group gathered.

Collaborative tasks, pitched within the group's zone of proximal development, must be well designed to ensure that all pupils have an equal opportunity and expectation to contribute. No single pupil should be allowed to take over or sit back, and tasks should be carefully planned to include all pupils with special educational needs. Group size is important too, as the task and the workload can become fragmented if the group is too large. Friendship groups and personality clashes have to be considered as well, if the experience is to be productive for everyone. With all these considerations, plus the fact that group work means ceding control over what pupils do and learn, it is not surprising that teachers underuse collaborative group work for organising learning (Baines *et al.*, 2015).

An added factor is that, when a TA is present, pupils tend to look to the TA to mediate the activity, rather than manage it themselves. Pupils will check ideas or ways forward with the TA, rather than discussing things with each other. This works against the express intention of collaborative group work, which is that the group learns to regulate itself.

TAs have a key role here to support effective group work and facilitate interactions – but not in the way pupils might expect. Your role is to ensure that it is the pupils that take the lead, interact with one another and work as a team to achieve the outcome. You are, in a sense, scaffolding the learning of group work skills. The skills required to do this are additional to those needed to directly support pupils (which we have covered in the previous chapters), but are still based on careful observation and intervening at the right moment to ensure that the group works as independently as possible towards its goal. The fostering of pupil independence is a guiding principle underpinning the SPRinG approach.

Another of SPRinG's guiding principles is that pupils need to have an understanding of good group work skills; that is, how to participate, take turns, teamwork, etc. These very learnable skills have to be developed over time. Pupils cannot just be put into groups and be expected to work well together. This is where TAs, as expert scaffolders, come in: they are key to helping teachers ensure that pupils develop group work skills and take responsibility for their learning and outcomes.

In the early years, initial group work skills need to be planned alongside the subject content of adult-scaffolded groups. As pupils get exposed to more group-based activities, they should be able to carry out collaborative tasks with increasing levels of autonomy. The idea, of course, is to limit adult interventions; prompt sheets or guidelines posted on the wall might be useful to help pupils who tend to look to you for help.

Eventually, group work skills can be used and practised alongside subject content. The implication for teachers, however, is that their early attempts are likely to be somewhat experimental. It is important that teachers 'hold firm' and use these opportunities to embed group work principles and skills, rather than overly concern themselves with achieving perfect learning outcomes (Baines *et al.*, 2015). Again, your role as observer and provider of detailed feedback is absolutely invaluable. Teachers will need quality feedback on which features of the task and group dynamics worked well and which require improvement, if they are to continue using collaborative group work.

Supporting collaborative group work

The SPRinG project was designed to help teachers teach pupils the skills needed for effective collaborative group work. It was structured to work first on social skills, then communication skills and, finally, collaborative problem-solving. The project led to a handbook by Baines *et al.* (2009), which provides practical activities and guidance to support the development of these skills. You can find information about the project and download resources and materials at www.spring-project.org.uk. Below, we have summarised some of the specific skills that the SPRinG approach can help to develop, and how you can support this.

Social skills

TRUST AND RESPECT

Mutual trust and respect are the foundation of effective group work. It can, of course, take time to build trust in other people, so it is recommended that, in the initial stages, pupils work consistently in the same groups. There are lots of games and exercises that can be used to develop trust. A key learning aim is for pupils to recognise and respect that others have views that differ from their own. They must learn that others are entitled to own and express these views. TAs can ensure the values of trust and respect are upheld by group members, and intervene if discussions turn into squabbles (see 'Avoiding disputes' below).

Having a set of 'group talk rules', agreed by everyone in the class, can be helpful in setting the groundwork. Both the SPRinG and Thinking Together materials (which we discuss later) have examples of rules for group talk. It is advisable to develop the rules *with* the pupils, and these should mirror any similar rules or expectations set by the teacher for interactions in other contexts (e.g. whole-class settings). This is important because pupils will eventually work as groups with other classmates, so all group work should be underpinned by a consistent set of rules.

REFLECTION ACTIVITY

Do the classrooms you work in have rules for when pupils work as groups?

Are the rules readily available to pupils as they work (e.g. posted on the wall) and do pupils refer to them?

Do you refer the pupils to these rules when you are supporting a collaborative task?

What are the key features of a set of group talk rules?

Communication skills

LISTENING

Pupils are expected to actively listening when others are speaking. Listeners must allow the speaker time and space to express themselves and develop their points. Setting an expectation that pupils might be asked to summarise what another has said is a helpful strategy for developing this skill, perhaps with the aid of notes. Pupils will also need to react to what is being said, so additional points to note could include:

- things that they want to find out more about;
- anything that is not clear or that they want to clarify;
- things that they agree with;
- things that they do not agree with, and why.

EXPLAINING

It is important that pupils are able to explain their ideas, views and thinking. On occasions, their explanations might be incomplete or require extension. A useful strategy here, as the guide on the side, is to simply ask the question 'why?' This can prompt a pupil to elaborate on their idea, so the group has a clearer understanding of their thinking. This is a skill that you can help pupils to develop in everyday situations. With the zone of proximal development in mind, encourage pupils to start from what they know. For example, you might ask them to explain a game they play in the playground, or why they chose a particular material to make a model. The key word to encourage pupils to use is 'because'. You can use this word as a prompt to encourage pupils to develop their ideas and think more deeply about their choices and the justifications for their views, and to open up the possibility that alternative choices and views might be available for consideration. In time, pupils will start to use 'because' as a strong connective in both their speaking and their writing, without the need for prompting.

AVOIDING DISPUTES

Establishing a respectful environment for group work takes time, but pupils need to learn that what they do or say can lead to upset or even conflict, albeit unintentionally. One pupil's valid view might offend the sensibilities of another. In some extreme cases, there will be procedures for addressing particularly offensive viewpoints in line with school policy. Far more commonplace are the situations where the views and ideas of one pupil might be considered by others to be controversial or 'wrong'; for example, in a discussion about capital punishment, one pupil might be against the death penalty, while the others are strongly in favour and are less accepting of their classmate's position.

Sometimes, constructive debates lead to heated exchanges. Teachers should be mindful of this and organise each group so it contains at least one pupil who can be a calming influence. Of course, all pupils need to regulate themselves and also take responsibility for the group's actions overall, so they need to recognise when things are getting heated and how to de-escalate the situation. The group talk rules give a reference point for this and, from your position on the side, you can remind pupils of these expectations if you feel the group is failing to manage itself. Other techniques, especially with younger pupils, might include reminders to look at the person who is talking, ensure fair and equal turn-taking and make sure that stronger personalities do not dominate. For older pupils, examples include reinforcing the expectations around respect, actively listening to everybody's ideas and taking notes so that they can respond fully when it is their turn to speak.

Collaborative problem-solving

ORGANISING THE GROUP AND PLANNING TASKS

Collaborative tasks require the group to organise itself and to plan what to do. Anyone who has ever worked in classrooms where pupils do not have good group work skills will know that this can be a task in itself! When pupils start to work collaboratively, it might be necessary to allocate roles to the members of the group. As you do this, it is important to explain why each member has been given his or her specific role. For example, you might say: 'I'm going to make Jake the scribe because he is good at noting the most important things that people say'; or 'I am giving Nadia the role of chairperson because it would be good for her to practise her leadership skills'. Depending on the task, you might nominate a 'timekeeper', a 'collector' (someone who gathers resources), a 'trouble-shooter' (someone who can think of ways to solve problems) or a 'researcher' (someone who can find things out while the group continues to work).

Similar principles apply while planning the task. Initially, you might provide the group with the process success criteria and suggest how long each stage should take to complete in order to aid time management. Over time, the responsibility for deciding roles democratically and planning what to do will be fully transferred to the pupils. However, like the other group work skills, this requires time and opportunities to practise. Getting these things right means that pupils can eventually give full focus to the learning task. It is important not to underestimate the value of learning the basics of organising and planning, which adults can take for granted.

Perhaps the most important conclusion from the SPRinG project is that there needs to be discussion about the collaborative group work skills that pupils are developing *as they work*. This is reminiscent of the learning commentaries we discussed in Chapter 4. As you observe the group working together, you can highlight the particular skills and processes they are demonstrating in their contribution to the outcome (e.g. praising them when they reach a compromise). At the outset of collaborative experiences, these skills can also be set out in the process success criteria. For example:

- Agree the ground rules for discussion.
- Allocate a role for each person.
- Make a plan of action.
- Check everybody has shared their ideas with the group.

These are just four examples of process success criteria that attend to the development of group work skills, but once these foundations are in place, the criteria will relate to learning and other skills teachers need members of the group to develop. So, in a lesson exploring fairness and equality, for example, a group might be asked to decide which employees of a company deserve a pay rise. Each person in the group must take on a role (e.g. the company director; a shareholder; a highly paid employee; a low-paid employee; the low-paid employee's spouse, etc.), find a way to present their case for the pay rise and then step outside of their roles to reach a consensus about who (if anyone) gets more money. At the end of the activity, the process success criteria can be assessed with the pupils and then used to develop new criteria for the next task.

SHARING IDEAS

All pupils should be prepared to contribute to the group effort and share their ideas. For some pupils, this can be a challenge. This might mean that groups need to allow more time for some members to fully participate. For example, allowing a little longer for some pupils to think through their ideas can benefit everyone else in the group. As we described above, some pupils might find it useful to rehearse what they want to say with you before presenting their thoughts to the group. Again, the group talk rules can accommodate this. Many schools use the 'talk partners' strategy to encourage less confident pupils to share ideas, and this can be imported into group work. Partners must be carefully selected, and if at first the partner is the TA, it will be important to build up the pupil's confidence quickly so that they are able and comfortable to work with a peer in future.

MAKING GROUP DECISIONS

Collaborative tasks have an outcome that must be arrived at with the consent of the whole group. Of course, nobody likes to have their ideas rejected, but it is important that this does not lead to ill-feeling or trigger a dispute. It is, for understandable reasons, these kinds of issues that make many teachers wary of collaborative group work. What is equally understood, however, is how collaborative group work provides the best context for developing and practising the essential skills needed for group participation and learning about the processes of democratic decision-making. Agreeing a compromise or changing one's mind are outcomes that should be positively pursued and praised. Indeed, when you see that a pupil is making an effort to compromise or has rethought their position (or reorganised their schema) in light of new information generated by the group, you can alert the rest of the group to this and draw attention to the value this has to the task goal.

REFLECTION ACTIVITY

Think about the most recent group activities or paired work you supported.

If there were any process success criteria, did they relate to the type of group work skills we have explored in this chapter?

Can you identify the group work skills the pupils you work with need to develop?

How could you help them develop these skills?

Developing exploratory talk

We can see evidence of the group work skills from the SPRinG project in the three kinds of talk you might hear when pupils are carrying out collaborative tasks: cumulative talk, disputational talk and exploratory talk (Mercer, 1995). Cumulative talk describes situations where pupils are working well together, but are simply agreeing with one another rather than discussing alternative scenarios and possible viewpoints; there is an absence of deep questioning. Disputational talk is characterised by pupils' failure to put forward the reasons for disagreeing with what someone else says; they do not extend their initial thoughts. When this happens, there is greater room for unconstructive forms of disagreement and it becomes difficult to reach a consensus. High occurrences of cumulative talk and disputational talk are unhelpful and mean that pupils are less likely to develop and practise critical thinking and reasoning skills.

The third of Mercer's talk types is, by contrast, far more helpful in the development of these crucial learning and life skills. Exploratory talk draws on Vygotsky's notion of 'thinking together'. Pupils talk through the ideas that emerge from group discussion. There is likely to be agreement and disagreement as different points of view are shared, but this all happens in a positive way. Pupils are respectful of opinions that differ from their own and recognise that these different views might exist in the wider world, even if none of the group members actually hold them. Alternative ideas are put forward, along with the reasons for and against, or the pros and cons, and debated openly. Pupils are supportive when a member of the group appears to change their mind in light of new information. Everybody approaches decision-making with an open mind and flexibility, as the group outcome is prioritised over personal agendas.

REFLECTION ACTIVITY

Observe a small group of pupils (fewer than five) working together on a collaborative task. Using the table below, make a tally of instances under the three 'talk type' headings. Do this for a short period of time (i.e. no more than five minutes). As you go, write down some examples of each talk type.

Look at your results. What are the characteristics of each type of talk? Are they any key words?

Even better, make a video or audio recording. On the first viewing, complete the tally and, on the second viewing, look for examples.

Cumulative talk	Disputational talk	Exploratory talk
Tally	Tally	Tally
Examples	Examples	Examples

As we mentioned above, pupils differ in the extent to which they have the skills to work effectively as part of a group. As part of the drive to improve *all* pupils' group work skills, teachers should ensure that there are opportunities to develop exploratory talk skills. We have already discussed a number of strategies for achieving this, but the trick is that this has to happen within the context of a collaborative task.

Collaborative tasks are a proven vehicle for developing group work skills and exploratory talk (Baines *et al.*, 2015). To extend this metaphor, without providing opportunities to practise these skills by setting collaborative tasks, it is like trying to learn to drive without getting behind the wheel of a car. When pupils are able to work collaboratively and engage in exploratory talk, there is less need for adult intervention and support; plus, there can be a knock-on effect in terms of attainment. Groups, on the other hand, whose members are unwilling to challenge each other's thinking, or who argue, are not working in conditions conducive to improving group work skills or attainment; plus, they are more likely to require adult supervision and intervention.

If the SPRinG principles are helpful for setting the right context and climate for group work, then the concept of exploratory talk forces us to focus on what pupils are saying and how their contributions build meaningfully on what other group members say. If exploratory talk is happening, you will hear words like: 'but', 'because' and 'why'. Perhaps you noted these key words as examples in the observation exercise above.

Over the last 20 years, primary and secondary schools have made good use of the practical activities and resources from the Thinking Together project led by Neil Mercer (http://thinkingtogether.educ.cam.ac.uk). This project teaches pupils to think together by developing their exploratory talk skills. Specific features of exploratory talk typically show evidence of active listening. Examples include:

- asking a good question;
- backing up a view or idea with a valid reason;
- challenging or probing an idea or suggestion (e.g. asking 'why?');
- asking for more information to support or extend an idea;
- developing someone else's idea;
- recognising the existence of other views in the group or the wider world;
- changing one's opinion;
- contributing relevant information;
- making a useful suggestion;
- making an interesting criticism;
- defusing a potential argument;
- facilitating the development of a consensus decision (e.g. showing leadership).

One of the best ways to support exploratory talk is to use video to help pupils study exactly what they say and how. Video also makes visible other important elements of interaction, such as facial expressions, gestures and actions. The recordings are used as the basis for a discussion about how pupils interact with each other, and how they can reduce their cumulative and disputational talk, and increase their exploratory talk.

REFLECTION ACTIVITY

Make a short video recording of a group at work. Replay the video and select a short section of no more than five minutes that contains a good range of the three main talk types.

Make copies of the tally table below (or make your own). Play the video to the group and ask them to make a tally of instances as they watch.

Ask the group to discuss their findings. Try using the following questions:

- *What can people do that makes group work go well?*
- *What makes group work go badly?*
- *What was the balance of helpful and unhelpful talk?*
- *How might these types of talk help the group reach their goal?*
- *Can you identify the features of helpful (exploratory) talk?*
- *How might you help yourself and others to increase helpful talk and reduce unhelpful talk?*

Examples of helpful talk	Examples of unhelpful talk
• Sharing information • Giving a good idea • Giving a reason for your view • Asking a good question • Building on what someone else says • Treating people with respect • Making sure everyone has a say	• Disagreeing without giving a reason • Too much agreement • Repeating/accepting ideas without challenge • Being competitive • Arguing or showing disrespect • Refusing to talk or disengaging
Tally	Tally

Summary

In this chapter, we have considered the ways in which pupils can work together both when working *in* a group, completing individual tasks, and when working *as* a group on a collaborative activity. We have discussed how you can support groups in subtle ways to ensure that the group retains ownership of the task and can manage itself effectively. We recognised that, in order to work as part of a group, all pupils need to develop good group work skills, and that these learnable skills are best practised through collaborative activities. Effective interaction within groups is essential to achieving collective aims. We therefore introduced the concept of exploratory talk as a way of helping pupils become attuned to the ways in which they interact with others and how this can affect group dynamics.

References

Baines, E., Blatchford, P. and Kutnick, P., with Chowne, A., Ota, C. and Berdondini, L. (2009) *Promoting effective group work in the primary classroom: A handbook for teachers and practitioners.* Oxon: Routledge.

Baines, E., Blatchford, P. and Webster, R. (2015) The challenges of implementing group work in primary school classrooms and including pupils with special educational needs. *Education 3–13: International Journal of Primary, Elementary and Early Years Education,* 43(1), pp. 15–23.

Blatchford, P., Russell, A. and Webster, R. (2012) *Reassessing the impact of teaching assistants: How research challenges practice and policy.* Oxon: Routledge.

Mercer, N. (1995) *The guided construction of knowledge: Talk amongst teachers and learners.* Clevedon: Multilingual Matters.

Webster, R. and Blatchford, P. (2013) The educational experiences of pupils with a Statement for special educational needs in mainstream primary schools. Results from a systematic observation study. *European Journal of Special Needs Education,* 28(4), pp. 463–479.

Further reading

Kutnick, P. and Blatchford, P. (2013) *Effective group work in primary school classrooms: The SPRinG approach.* Dordrecht: Springer.

Lefstein, A. and Snell, J. (2014) *Better than best practice: Developing teaching and learning through dialogue.* Oxon: Routledge.

Mercer, N. and Dawes, L. (2008) The value of exploratory talk. In N. Mercer and S. Hodgkinson (2008) (eds) *Exploring talk in school.* London: Sage.

Chapter 7

Delivering intervention programmes

In this chapter, we build on scaffolding and group work skills by exploring a particular, and very familiar, everyday context. Many TAs deliver intervention programmes designed to help pupils who have fallen behind in vital areas of learning or who are not attaining at the expected level. The most common interventions are for literacy: writing and spelling, phonics and developing reading skills. There are programmes to help children develop their mathematical skills. There are also 'non-curriculum' interventions for social skills and programmes to help children develop speech and language. It is common for all types of interventions to be delivered by TAs on a one-to-one or group basis, outside the classroom.

Here, we first discuss the types of interventions that are available to schools and the wider process of matching particular interventions to the needs of pupils. We then look at the importance of programme fidelity (delivering the programme as intended), subject knowledge and assessment and record-keeping. Finally, we consider the importance of linking the learning from intervention sessions to learning in the classroom.

While TAs typically deliver the intervention sessions, we know that the responsibility for selecting programmes, planning tasks and assessing pupils' work tends to be in the hands of teachers. The SEN Code of Practice indicates that teachers, under the guidance of the SENCO, have the overall responsibility for planning and organising intervention tasks. In this sense, intervention tasks are treated as no different to all other learning tasks for which teachers are responsible. That said, we also know that TAs are often involved, at least to some extent, in all or some of these activities. Accountability is important here, so throughout this chapter, we emphasise the specific role and responsibilities of teachers in relation to interventions.

What is an intervention programme?

For the purposes of this chapter, we define intervention programmes in a way that all readers will recognise. Intervention programmes (sometimes known as 'catch-up' or 'booster' programmes) are highly structured courses of input designed to supplement classroom teaching and achieve specific leaning outcomes. Many programmes are commercially available 'off the shelf'. A strong feature of these programmes is that they are 'time fixed'; that is, there is a directed timetable for the delivery of sessions, and the frequency and duration of the sessions are also specified. This is because programmes are designed to boost attainment in a relatively short period and limit as far as possible the amount of time pupils have to spend outside mainstream curriculum coverage.

Intervention programmes also define the specific set of knowledge and skills to be learned or developed by the end of the course. Off-the-shelf interventions provide materials and resources for pupils and adults, including worksheets, screening and assessment tools, delivery scripts and instructions. This provides clarity over what learning must be covered in each session. Finally, each intervention has its own protocols. It will have been designed to be delivered to individuals or groups and may specify a maximum group size. A 'target audience' might also be defined in terms of an age range or attainment range (e.g. for pupils achieving below a given threshold).

REFLECTION ACTIVITY

What intervention programmes are used in your school?

What intervention programmes (if any) do you teach?

When is an intervention used?

There are various reasons why an intervention might be put in place, and these decisions are taken on the basis of pupil need. Teachers carefully track pupils' developmental progress and make regular assessments of their attainment. School leaders monitor teachers' tracking and assessment to verify the accuracy of these assessments and teachers' recommendations of which pupils could benefit from an intervention programme.

According to the SEN Code of Practice, pupils in the frame for interventions will be those who are making less than the expected level of progress 'given their age and individual circumstances' (DfE/DoH, 2015, p. 95). The Code highlights the need for good tracking and early action, so that a school intervenes quickly when a dip in progress is identified. The longer it is before learning difficulties are tackled, the further behind the pupil is likely to fall. This, in turn, makes it increasingly difficult for them to catch up, and the gap between where they are now and where they need to be widens; so too will the gap between those who have fallen behind and their peers. Good tracking and assessment, coupled with the identification and implementation of strong intervention programmes, can ensure that pupils' needs are met before they fall too far behind.

Important though academic progress is, schools must also apply the same approach to other areas of pupil development. For example, pupils need to develop good social skills in order to thrive in school and in adult life. The Early Years Framework tracks all areas of development for every child, but beyond the infant years, the ways in which schools accurately measure the development of social skills are not so systematic. Even so, infant and primary schools do identify pupils who could benefit from an intervention to help develop good peer relations, and there are off-the-shelf packages designed for this purpose.

Yet in secondary education – where the focus tends to be more on academic progress – such interventions are rare. This might be because, by the time pupils reach secondary school, perceived weaknesses in social skills (such as a once outgoing pupil becoming withdrawn, or difficulty maintaining peer relations) tend to be construed as symptoms of SEN or a well-being issue. Because of this, they are likely to be managed in different ways.

An important point to make here is that pupils at any stage of education may be included in an intervention programme, and that such programmes are not exclusively for pupils with SEN. There are many reasons why a pupil might fall behind at moments during their school career (for example, a bereavement will affect performance for a while), but this does not mean that they have SEN. However, it is important to recognise that this *may* be the reason, and school monitoring and tracking systems led by SENCOs are designed to identify any pupils who might have an 'unidentified' SEN. Often, evidence of performance progress from intervention programmes is used as part of statutory assessment.

A final important point to make before we proceed is that, as pupils are typically withdrawn from class for interventions, so it should be a prerequisite of any programme that it *at least* compensates for time spent away from teacher-led instruction. Crucially though, this does not mean that the responsibility for pupils making accelerated progress falls to TAs.

REFLECTION ACTIVITY

How are pupils tracked in your school? Is there an electronic system for logging and tracking pupil data?

Who is responsible for flagging up concerns over pupil progress and how are these dealt with?

What makes an intervention programme successful?

Whether an intervention programme has been designed to support pupils to catch up or assist a pupil with a specific SEN or other need, the principles of what makes a programme successful are broadly the same. The SEN Code of Practice makes it clear that schools have a responsibility to ensure that approaches to improving learning outcomes are 'based on the best possible evidence' (DfE/DoH, 2015, p. 25). This applies to the identification and implementation of intervention programmes. The Code of Practice also makes it clear that the responsibility for this lies with the school leadership team, not TAs.

For this reason, there is a layer of detail that we need not go into here; interested readers can instead refer to *Maximising the Impact of Teaching Assistants* (Webster, Russell and Blatchford, 2016). It is, however, worth highlighting a few key points in relation to 'evidence-based approaches'. Simply put, 'evidence-based approaches' are things that have been shown to work. The Education Endowment Foundation (EEF) (www.educationendowmentfoundation.org.uk) is one of the UK's leading funders of research and has scrutinised which interventions do and do not help to raise attainment. The EEF recommend that schools use only intervention programmes that have been independently evaluated and show a demonstrable effect on attainment. It also suggests that schools abandon programmes for which there is no evidence of any effect on attainment (Sharples, Webster and Blatchford, 2015). Broadly speaking, the EEF reports that TA-led interventions have been shown to boost pupil progress by three to four additional months over an academic year. But crucially, these positive effects are *only* observed when TAs are used in structured settings with high-quality support and training. Given that there are decisions regarding intervention programmes that fall within the remit of school leaders, SENCOs and teachers, what can TAs do to ensure that intervention programmes are successful? Below, we consider three areas: programme fidelity, subject knowledge and assessment and record-keeping.

Fidelity to the programme

Another consistent lesson from the research on interventions tells us that one of the keys to success is fidelity to the programme; in other words, doing what it says on the label! The best programmes have been developed through studying theories about learning and how children acquire the foundations of knowledge and skills they need in order to succeed at more advanced levels. The programmes will have been tested and refined before being made available to schools; this is especially the case for commercial programmes. Careful testing, and evaluations by independent assessors, will have been conducted on the basis that the intervention has been delivered as its creators intended. For example, an intervention might state that it should be delivered three times a week, for 20 minutes, to groups of four pupils. So if schools want to achieve similar results to those reported in testing and evaluation, it is essential that they deliver the programme in *exactly* the same way and do not tinker with these essential factors; for example, delivering it to groups of six pupils, twice a week. If changes are made to any part of the programme, the programme itself changes, and the chances of success diminish. Points to remember include:

- If the intervention programme comes with a 'script', you need to use it as it is written.
- If resources are provided, use them as directed.
- If a duration is specified for each session or task, you need to keep to this timing.
- If a group size is specified, resist the temptation to include more pupils.
- If an intervention should be delivered on a one-to-one basis, do not use it with groups.

If you have any concerns – for example, if you think a particular session plan is not appropriate for the pupils – discuss this with the teacher. Sometimes intervention programmes are less tightly structured. There may be broad overviews of sessions, tasks and learning outcomes, but not specific scripts or resources; for example, there may be a suggestion that the group read a short story, but it does not specify a particular text. In such instances, consult the teacher. Remember: it is the teacher who has responsibility for the planning for *all* pupils, including those in intervention sessions.

It is helpful to have an outside view of your practice now and then to ensure you are being faithful to the delivery protocols of the programme. Try to ensure that you are regularly observed delivering the programme by somebody who is familiar with it. This objective view of your practice provides a useful opportunity to receive feedback and discuss any areas for improvement.

Subject knowledge

Good subject knowledge allows TAs to identify exactly when pupils are having difficulties and scaffold their learning effectively, avoiding any misconceptions. Subject knowledge does not just mean 'knowing facts', but knowing processes too. Let us take a common example. Bryn has been given a set of numbers and asked to multiply each one by ten. The TA has suggested that, to achieve this goal, all Bryn has to do is to write a zero to the right of each digit. Bryn gets each of these sums correct, but has he understood the process of multiplying numbers by ten? This may be a handy hint, but it only works for whole numbers, not decimals. Bryn really needs to observe the effect of multiplying by ten if he is to develop the depth of understanding needed to work successfully with decimal numbers.

Schools that are truly investing in their TA workforce should be providing regular opportunities for you to improve and develop your subject knowledge. But there are always things you can do to be proactive, such as making subject knowledge one of your performance management targets and identifying training or refresher courses to attend, linked to the interventions you deliver. You can always talk to subject specialists in your school to iron out any misconceptions you have about subject content. This is nothing to be embarrassed about; teachers constantly have to keep up to date with new teaching methods linked to the curriculum, so they will understand! Many TAs do self-directed study. The key thing to remember is to use materials that are compatible with the content and teaching methods used in the interventions you deliver. Many of the commercial programmes have websites with resources and videos, and you can always consult with teachers and SENCOs to find appropriate materials.

Assessment and record-keeping

Once a specific intervention has been identified as appropriate for meeting the needs of a particular pupil, it is usual to conduct some form of diagnostic assessment prior to the first session. Most commercial programmes come with some form of initial assessment or benchmarking tool to take a baseline measure of pupils' knowledge or attainment at the start of the programme. These assessments are narrowed to the specific set of knowledge or skills the intervention is designed to develop, so the initial assessment will test pupils' understanding and ability in these areas. Although you may be asked to carry out these initial assessments, and possibly conduct tests during and at the end of interventions, there should be no expectation that you select which pupils take part in the intervention sessions that follow.

It is teachers, of course, who are accountable for the outcomes from interventions, but as they are very often not those delivering the sessions, it is essential that you provide them with detailed feedback to aid their decision-making. Teachers should set the framework for feedback, ideally using any resources provided with the intervention package, but the alternative forms of record-keeping discussed in Chapter 5 could be used instead. Use these tools to flag any concerns about pupils' engagement, understanding and progress to teachers as early as possible. A pupil's failure to make progress in an intervention may be the result of an unidentified learning difficulty, and while it is up to the teacher and SENCO to decide what further action might be needed, your feedback could avoid any unnecessary delay to ensuring the pupil receives the specific provision their needs require.

As we have said elsewhere in this book, although it often feels like it, you do not bear personal responsibility for ensuring that pupils make progress in interventions. Naturally, you will make every effort to ensure that this happens, but it is important to recognise that there are factors and processes outside of your control that go a long way to ensuring pupils prosper from intervention sessions you lead, and it is up to school leaders and teachers to put this in place.

At the end of the programme, there is often some form of final assessment. Data collected through this test will be used to assess discrete levels of progress made during an intervention. To make the tests fair, the final assessment will have similar, if not the same, questions and tasks as the initial assessment; for example, decoding a set of words. Again, you might be asked to conduct these tests.

The SEN Code of Practice stresses the right of pupils with SEN to express their views about their learning, the provisions put in place to meet their needs and any further provisions they might need. We argue that this is good practice for all pupils, and appropriate not just at the end of an intervention, but at points during it too. So, as part of the assessments, you could ask pupils questions such as:

- How is the programme helping you? How has the programme helped you?
- What can you do now that you could not do at the start of the programme?
- Is there anything you need help with?
- What could help you to overcome this problem?
- Is there anyone in the intervention group who is having/has had the same problem who could help?

Linking learning in intervention sessions with learning in the classroom

The research evidence shows that interventions tend to be delivered separate from classroom activities. This, and the lack of time there often is for teachers and TAs to liaise with each other, means there is relatively little connection between what pupils experience in and away from the classroom. So it is often left to pupils to make links between the content of the intervention and the wider curriculum coverage back in the classroom. An anecdote from our own practice highlights the problem of bridging between the two contexts that schools need to address.

A colleague was once shadowing a Year 4 boy who had high-level SEN (let's call him Finley). She followed Finley and the TA who supported him when they went out of the classroom to do an intervention session in the library. The focus of the session was the use of full stops. Finley received some instruction from the TA on the use of full stops, and then diligently undertook an exercise in which he correctly completed each short sentence with a full stop. Back in the classroom, no more than an hour later, our colleague was puzzled to see Finley writing sentences without putting a full stop at the end. When she asked why, Finley replied, quite innocently: 'I do my full stops in the library with my TA'.

Given that the pupils who are targeted for interventions (like Finley) tend to find accessing learning difficult in the first place, the integration of the specific intervention with the mainstream curriculum is therefore vital; as such, it is one of the critical areas for action covered in *Maximising the Impact of Teaching Assistants* (Webster et al., 2016). It is suggested that, in secondary schools, giving English and maths departments the responsibility for co-ordinating intervention programmes can help ensure teachers have full control of the factors they need in order to plan effective provision. In other words, key inputs relating to literacy and numeracy basics do not become seen as 'the responsibility of the Learning Support department'. In primary schools, teachers should be supported to capitalise on TA-led learning by aligning the content of strategically selected intervention programmes with wider curriculum coverage of literacy and numeracy.

These broader school actions mean it is more likely that TAs are in a better position to help 'lock in' the learning from intervention sessions. Of course, the most effective way to do this is to use the scaffolding framework to prompt or clue pupils to draw on the strategies, techniques, skills and knowledge from the programmes.

It is important to recognise and praise pupils when they make connections and apply learning from interventions in classroom contexts (e.g. during group work or teacher-led input) – all the more so if they do this unprompted (in other words, they are self-scaffolding). It is necessary to record and feed back these instances to teachers, together with any missed opportunities; that is, instances where pupils failed to make the connections, despite reasonable support from you.

Summary

In this chapter, we have addressed some key issues in relation to how TAs are deployed to deliver intervention programmes for pupils who have fallen behind. We have clarified what interventions are and how they should be used, together with key features of successful programmes. We explored some of the main points to consider when linking learning from intervention sessions to teaching and learning back in the classroom. We have been careful throughout to avoid any suggestion that TAs are accountable for the outcomes of interventions, in terms of wider pupil progress. It is teachers who are responsible for *all* outcomes for *all* pupils in *all* contexts. As such, they must have the responsibility for planning and organising interventions tasks, as they do for learning tasks in their classrooms. But feedback from TAs is, of course, essential to quality planning.

References

Department for Education and Department of Health (2015) *Special educational needs and disability code of practice: 0 to 25 years. Statutory guidance for organisations which work with and support children and young people who have special educational needs or disabilities.* Available online at: www.gov.uk/government/uploads/system/uploads/attachment_data/file/398815/SEND_Code_of_Practice_January_2015.pdf (accessed 20 February 2015).

Sharples, J., Webster, R. and Blatchford, P. (2015) Making best use of teaching assistants. Guidance report – March 2015. London: Education Endowment Foundation. Available online at: https://educationendowmentfoundation.org.uk/uploads/pdf/Making_best_use_of_TAs_printable.pdf (accessed 10 July 2015).

Webster, R., Russell, A. and Blatchford, P. (2016) *Maximising the impact of teaching assistants: Guidance for school leaders and teachers*, second edition. Oxon: Routledge.

Conclusion

A summary of coverage

In this book, we have presented a case for a complementary and distinct role for teaching assistants, one that has the potential to add real value to teachers and contribute to schools' overall drive to raise standards and achievement. The pivotal findings from the large-scale Deployment and Impact of Support Staff (DISS) project made it clear that schools need to fundamentally rethink their use of TAs (Blatchford, Russell and Webster, 2012). This, together with our further research, has revealed that the quality of pupils' learning is dependent on schools working through a clear and consistent role for both TAs and teachers. Having a shared understanding of one another's role and the best ways to work together to support pupils' needs is critical to providing the best possible learning experience.

Obviously, the responsibility for undertaking this rethink falls to school leaders; the DISS project was clear that it is the decisions made *about* TAs, not *by* TAs, that are at the root of ineffective uses of TAs. A framework for action directed at school leaders is detailed in the companion book, *Maximising the Impact of Teaching Assistants* (Webster, Russell and Blatchford, 2016). What was needed alongside this book was guidance specifically for TAs on how to develop their practice on the ground. It has been the express aim of this book to provide a framework for effective scaffolding, underpinned by a theoretical grounding, which builds on (yet is consistent with) the school-level process set out in the companion book.

A starting point for our book is the recognition that, while many TAs have a pedagogical role, there is often inconsistency in their approaches to scaffolding. We have sought to fill this gap by providing help for TAs to develop a role for themselves as an 'expert scaffolder'. Another clear aim of our guidance has been to attend to the problems associated with 'learned helplessness', which pupils often develop when intensive adult support is readily available. Therefore, our book has also focused on how you can develop pupils' independence through the way you talk with them. As you will no doubt have noticed, these are self-supporting aims and processes. You should now be well on the way to equipping yourself with the skills to help pupils to self-scaffold their learning and to build within learners the capacity to become more confident and secure in their ability to take responsibility for their own learning.

Good scaffolding starts from knowing the steps, or key components, needed to complete a task. With the task broken up into 'mini-goals' (process success criteria), TAs can provide meaningful support by:

- observing self-scaffolding and pupils' attempts to problem-solve;
- providing a prompt to help pupils remember general problem-solving techniques and to give encouragement and praise for effort and perseverance;
- providing a clue to help them bring to mind particular learning strategies or a piece of information;
- modelling a particular part of the task, demonstrating how to do something pupils are expected to try for themselves next time.

It is important to start from the position that pupils can, and should, carry out tasks as independently as possible (that is, self-scaffold). We have encouraged you to adopt the approach of giving the least amount of help first. Observing and listening carefully as pupils are working supports contingency, whereby you respond to what the pupil has just said or done. Hard though it sometimes is, your first response should be to do nothing. Intervene only when the pupil demonstrates a clear need for a verbal or visual prompt. Clues follow prompts, and modelling follows clueing. Except when pupils have exceptional needs and the use is planned (e.g. a speech and language programme), avoid any temptation to provide the answer or to correct.

Your role is, of course, far from passive. But by stepping back in this way, you not only encourage pupil independence, but allow space for peer interaction and group work. What is more, it provides you with the opportunity to record feedback for teachers, which is an essential component of good assessment for learning.

The *Maximising the Impact of Teaching Assistants* approach stresses that changing practice in schools is a long game. This can also be the case at the pupil level. A particular challenge you may face is helping to move pupils towards a growth mindset, where what they learn about their learning matters at least as much as – if not more than – the completion of the task. As pupils become more confident and able to give honest appraisals of their learning, you can build further on the best principles of assessment for learning by involving them in evaluating their progress towards independent working.

This book has provided opportunities for reflecting on your practice and maintaining an on-going record of how your practice develops as you work through and embed the ideas and strategies we describe. We would encourage you to redo the self-evaluation in Chapter 1 at regular points along *your* learning journey and to update your continuing professional development planner as you do so.

Evidence of impact

As you worked through this book, you may have asked yourself whether the approaches and strategies we have set out actually work. What is the evidence that changing how you interact with pupils improves things for you and them? The first thing to say about this is that TA–pupil interaction is a fairly new area of research, and to date, there are very few studies that have examined impact. What we can say is that the research evidence is clear on the types of talk that are ineffective: talk that does not help pupils to become independent or hampers their learning. So logically, if we dramatically reduce the use of these practices and introduce techniques that we know work when teachers use them, we at least create the conditions in which we might expect to find an impact on pupils' sense of responsibility for their own leaning and learning itself, in terms of improved attainment.

We have seen improvements in TAs' practice in the work we have undertaken with schools. For example, in the Effective Deployment of TAs (EDTA) project (Webster *et al.*, 2016), there was good work by schools on changing TAs' talk with pupils, which included encouraging TAs to consider when *not* to talk, thereby giving pupils time to think and attempt tasks for themselves. We saw evidence that TAs were encouraged to adopt the principle that interactions with pupils should be about understanding, not task completion. Questioning frameworks were introduced to help pupils remain in charge of, and responsible for, their own learning, and thereby reduce dependency on adult support. TA practice also developed to support formative assessment. In terms of the impact on TAs, it was clear that those who took part in the EDTA project felt more valued and appreciated by their school, and more confident in their role and abilities.

In the schools that developed the specific activities and materials contained in this book, the scaffolding framework is used by TAs, pupils and teachers, and has led to a whole-school focus on independence and self-scaffolding. Parents have also become part of this conversation; all the strategies used in school work equally well for everyday activities at home, such as a child making sure that they have everything they need ready for the next school day. Headteachers report findings from TA observations showing that pupils are being given more thinking time, more open questions are being used and the focus of interactions has moved to the learning rather than task completion. Perhaps the most important change is that pupils are using the language of independence themselves: they say 'I am going to self-scaffold by getting a dictionary to check that word'. It is encouraging that pupils are being given space to try things for themselves, to make mistakes and to talk about what they have learned from the process.

Final word

We have spent a number of years working with TAs in a variety of schools. The vast majority of TAs we meet are hard-working, highly committed to pupils' learning and well-being, good humoured and keen to develop their practice. We see enormous potential in the TA workforce within schools. Our aim is to ensure that schools release this untapped potential, and that TAs themselves are well informed, well trained and able to reflect meaningfully on their practice and have the skills to know how to improve what they do. We see this book as a significant step towards realising this aim.

References

Blatchford, P., Russell, A. and Webster, R. (2012) *Reassessing the impact of teaching assistants: How research challenges practice and policy.* Oxon: Routledge.

Webster, R., Russell, A. and Blatchford, P. (2016) *Maximising the impact of teaching assistants: Guidance for school leaders and teachers*, second edition. Oxon: Routledge.

Appendices

Planning for changes to practice

	TA	Teachers	Line manager
Area to be adjusted	Changes to practice that will be observed (be specific – *I need to . . .*)	What do teachers need to do to support/manage this change?	What other support would help you to achieve this change?

Planning for changes to practice: completed example

	TA	Teachers	Line manager
Area to be adjusted	Changes to practice that will be observed (be specific – *I need to . . .*)	What do teachers need to do to support/manage this change?	What other support would help you to achieve this change?
Modelling (providing a commentary)	Use prompts and clues before modelling. Model only the specific part of the task that the pupil is stuck on. Use 'I' while demonstrating. Ask the pupil to carry out the steps immediately after modelling.	Provide clear modelling of the whole task as part of the whole-class input.	Line manager to carry out a focused observation on use of modelling.
Assessment for learning	Give specific feedback against each success criteria. Relate feedback to how independently the pupil completed the task.	Provide clear process success criteria.	Agreement over record-keeping format.
Linking phonics intervention sessions to learning in the classroom	During classroom tasks use prompts and clues which link to the intervention programme. Note when pupils are/are not transferring knowledge during classroom tasks and feed back to teacher.	Provide opportunities for pupils to practise intervention session skills in classroom tasks. Make clear references to phonic knowledge covered in intervention group sessions during whole-class/group input.	Highlight the importance of linking intervention sessions and classroom tasks to teachers.

©2016, *The Teaching Assistant's Guide to Effective Interaction*, Paula Bosanquet, Julie Radford and Rob Webster

Appendix 3

Commentary on extract

What examples of wait-time, self-scaffolding, prompting, clueing, modelling and correcting can you find?

1 TA: (*pointing at whiteboard*) Can you see where the head of the p sits?
2 Tim: (*nods head*)
3 TA: Where does he sit?———→ Prompting
4 Tim: (*points at p*)
5 (*three-second pause*)———→ Wait time
6 Tim: On the grass.   ↗ Modelling
7 TA: In the grass, OK? So.
8 Tim: And mine's in the sky ———→ Self-scaffolding
9 TA: Yeah, he's got his head in the sky, hasn't he? So if he's got his head
10   in the sky that means he's a capital p. And we don't want capital
11   p's because this p is at the end of lip. OK? So please try that one
12   again. (*starts to talk to another child*) How are we getting on? Oh,
13   they're beautiful. Well done.
14 Tim: Shall I put it here? ———→ Self-scaffolding
15 TA: What? Oh yeah. So if you stop. Oh yeah, they are tricky
16   ones. I'm going to do another one, just watch. So we're going
17   down, my tail's going into the ground. So it's descending, and then,
18   so the whole of the head of the p is in the grass.

(right margin, lines 9–11:) Modelling

(right margin, lines 15–18:) Modelling

Overall, how independent is this pupil being in this interaction?

Are there any parts where you would have done or said something different? Why?

There is clear evidence that Tim is able to self-scaffold. The TA uses a prompt in line 3 (repeating the question), which she follows with silence in line 5. Not saying anything in line 5 indicates to Tim that something else is needed and he gives more information in line 6, verbalising the position of the head of the p. So the silence in line 5 works as a prompt for Tim to extend his answer. However, rather than saying *in* the grass Tim has said *on* the grass. This is significant in relation to this particular task (the preposition is important for clarifying the exact position of the letter on the handwriting lines). So the TA recasts Tim's response, changing the *on* for *in*. There is an excellent example of self-scaffolding in line 8, with Tim self-correcting. He is able to say what is wrong about the p that he has already written. In lines 10 and 11, the TA takes Tim's self-correction and explains how the differences in position are linked

---

to upper and lower case letters. We would argue that clarifying the difference would have been better done through questioning. An example of a prompt question would be: 'It's in the sky. So what does that mean?' An example of a clue question would be: 'It's in the sky. So does that make it a capital p or a lower case p?' This could lead to further questions about the type of letter required.

There is a further example of self-scaffolding in line 14. Although Tim asks for help, he does it in a specific way. He indicates exactly what piece of information he needs confirmation for: 'Shall I put it here?' It is clear that Tim has not yet understood where to place the head of the p so the TA provides a model in lines 16–18. In terms of independence, a prompt or clue would have been preferable first. A prompt might be: 'Can you tell me why you think it starts there?' A clue might be: 'Do we want an upper case p or a lower case p?' If a model was then needed, we would suggest that the wording was changed to use 'I' rather than 'we' (line 16).

Assessment for learning sheet

Date: Subject: Class:

Write names/initials and the success criteria (you do not have to use all the boxes).

	Name	Name	Name	Name
Process success criteria				
1				
2				
3				
4				
5				

Key:

✓	Can do this independently
P	Can do with prompting
C	Can do with clues
M	Modelled for the child

Notes (e.g. useful resources, specific difficulties, useful prompts)

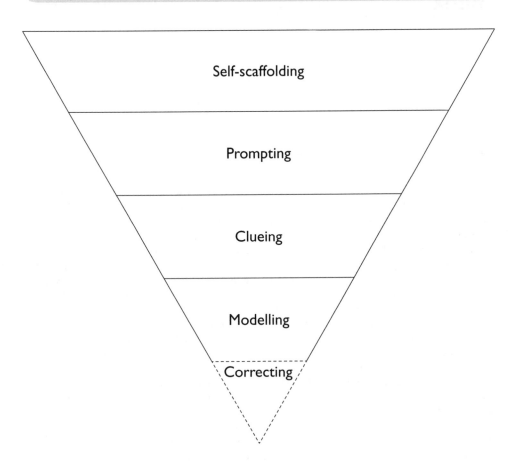

Self-scaffolding

Prompting

Clueing

Modelling

Correcting

Index

accountability 103
active listening 70, 71, 101
administrative support 4
Alexander, R. 35
asking for help 22, 62, 90–91
assessment: EDTA project 112; for learning 14, 18, 19, 76, 78–79, 81, 83–84, 87, 111, 115, 118; intervention programmes 104, 105, 107–108; of learning 76, 77–78, 79; planning for changes to practice 115; self-assessment 79, 84–87
assimilation 25
attainment: DISS project results 6; intervention programmes 103, 104, 105; *see also* performance
audio recordings 61, 72, 74

Baines, E. 92, 95
Bakhtin, Mikhail 26
behaviour support 5
Black, Paul 79, 83, 84
Blatchford, Peter 6, 8, 94
Bruner, J. S. 32, 44

characteristics of teaching assistants 7, 10
Clarke, Shirley 47
class-based support 3
classroom talk 33–34
closed questions 9, 35
clueing 53, 54, 59, 60, 66–68, 111; assessment for learning sheet 118; commentary on extract 117; giving feedback to teachers 82; intervention programmes 109; puppet technique 93; self-evaluation 18; studying your interactions 71–73
cognitive development 25, 26, 27, 31, 35
collaborative learning 94–99, 100, 102

commentary technique 45, 68–69, 86
communication skills 95, 96–97
comprehension 28
concept maps 25
conditions of employment 7, 10, 12
Confederation of British Industry (CBI) 11
confidence 20, 22, 23, 60, 87, 110; fixed mindset 40; peer support 89, 90, 93; prompts 65; self-assessment 86; 'talk partners' 98
constructivist learning theory 25–26; *see also* social constructivist learning theory
contingency 46–47, 52, 111; contingent teaching 32, 84
continuing professional development (CPD) 18
cooking 30
correcting 53, 55, 59, 70–71, 72–73
cover supervisors 4
cumulative talk 99, 100, 101

decision-making 99, 100
decoding 28
demotivation 41
deployment 7–8, 12, 13
Deployment and Impact of Support Staff (DISS) project 6–11, 19, 88, 110
diagnostic questions 46–47, 57, 84
diagnostic tests 77, 107
dialogic talk 34–37, 41
differentiation, definition of 44
digraphs 66–67
disability 3; *see also* special educational needs
disputational talk 99, 100, 101
disputes 97
DISS *see* Deployment and Impact of Support Staff project
Dweck, Carol 40

Education, Health and Care Plans (EHCPs) 86

Education Endowment Foundation (EEF) 105

Effective Deployment of TAs (EDTA) project 112

Emotional Literacy Support Assistants (ELSAs) 4–5

employment conditions 7, 10, 12

end-of-year reports 77

English as an Additional Language (EAL) 4, 55

evaluation: 'high level' 35; self-assessment 85; self-scaffolding 37, 38

evidence-based approaches 105

examinations 11, 77

explaining 96–97

exploratory talk 94, 99–102

faculty-based support 3

failure, fear of 22

feedback: assessment for learning 115; contingency 52; fixed mindset 41; giving feedback to pupils 83–84; giving feedback to TAs 12; giving feedback to teachers 20, 47, 75, 76, 79–83, 95, 109, 111; intervention programmes 106, 107; IRF pattern 33–34; mini-goals 48; scaffolding 19, 21, 41

fixed mindset 40–41, 89

Ford, Henry 40, 41

formative assessment 78, 112; see also assessment

formative feedback 83–84, 90

gestures 65–66, 72

Giangreco, Michael 10

goals 21, 31, 32; group work 94; pupil participation in setting 86; self-scaffolding 37; see also mini-goals; process success criteria

group work 14, 88–102; collaborative learning 94–99; exploratory talk 99–102; peer support 88–93; self-evaluation 18

growth mindset 40, 41, 46, 83, 86, 87, 89, 111

handwriting 45–46

headteachers 13, 112

help, definition of 44

heuristic role 20

heuristic scaffolding 38

higher-level teaching assistants (HLTAs) 1, 4

ideas, sharing 98

identity, professional 21

inclusion 19

independence 23, 45, 46, 52; assessment for learning sheet 118; commentary on extract 117; encouraging 62; giving feedback to teachers 76, 82, 83; group work 95; growth mindset 41; process success criteria 51, 78–79; scaffolding framework 22, 53, 59, 60, 74, 112; self-assessment 84, 85; self-evaluation 18; self-scaffolding 38, 54, 111; structured help 57; see also responsibility

instructions 55, 61, 62, 69, 118

intelligence 40

interaction 9, 20, 21, 41; classroom talk 33–34; peer 22, 90, 92, 93; scaffolding 47, 52, 53–55, 75; self-scaffolding 38; social constructivist learning theory 26, 27, 30; special educational needs 8; studying your interactions 71–74; zone of learning 32

'interthinking' 35

intervention programmes 4, 14, 103–109; assessment and record-keeping 107–108; definition of 103–104; linking to classroom learning 108–109, 115; programme fidelity 106; self-evaluation 18; subject knowledge 106–107; when they are used 104–105

IRF (Initiation, Response, Feedback) 33–34, 35, 36

jigsawing 94

knowledge: co-construction of 26; intervention programmes 104; knowledge pupils bring to a task 31; prior 63; subject 4, 9, 106–107; zone of proximal development 28

Kutnick, Peter 94

language: intervention programmes 4, 103; learning new words 70, 71; modelling 55

leading whole classes 4

learned helplessness 10–11, 110

learning: assessment for 14, 18, 19, 76, 78–79, 81, 83–84, 87, 111, 115, 118; assessment of 77–78, 79; collaborative 94–99, 100, 102; constructivist theory

25–26; how we learn 24–25; intervention programmes 108–109, 115; modelling 70; negative consequences of TAs on 6, 9; pupil's ownership over 86, 87, 89; relevance of 30–31; scaffolding framework 21–23; social constructivist theory 24, 25, 26–27, 30–31, 34; zone of 31–32
liaising with teachers 10, 12
listening: active 70, 71, 101; group work 96, 97
literacy 4, 77, 103, 108–109
'live feedback' 80–81

Making a Statement (MAST) study 8, 19, 88
maths 29, 40, 67, 69, 77, 103
Maximising the Impact of TAs (MITA) approach 11–13, 19
Maximising the Impact of Teaching Assistants (Webster, Russell and Blatchford, 2016) 2, 12, 21, 23, 105, 108, 110, 111
Mercer, Neil 32, 35, 94, 99, 101
metacognition 37, 69; *see also* self-scaffolding
mindsets: fixed mindset 40–41, 89; growth mindset 40, 41, 46, 83, 86, 87, 89, 111
mini-goals 31, 32, 47–52, 110; giving feedback to pupils 84; giving feedback to teachers 82; self-scaffolding 37, 38, 63; *see also* process success criteria
modelling 53, 55, 59, 68–70, 111; asking for help 90–91; assessment for learning sheet 118; commentary on extract 116, 117; giving feedback to teachers 82; planning for changes to practice 115; process success criteria 51, 57; puppet technique 93; self-assessment 85; self-evaluation 18; studying your interactions 71–73
motivation 32, 41, 64

non-pedagogical roles 3, 4–5
numeracy 4, 108–109
Nystrand, Martin 35

observation 57, 60, 62, 80–81, 111
one-to-one support 3, 7–8
open questions 9, 35, 112

parents 38, 41, 112
pastoral support 4–5
pedagogical roles 3–4, 5, 7, 12, 20, 110
peer support 22, 88–93

performance 76, 79, 105; *see also* attainment; progress
performance management 12, 107
persistence 22, 41, 111
phonics 4, 77, 103, 115
Piaget, Jean 25–26, 27
picture boards 62
planning: changes to practice 114–115; group work 98; independent learning 85; self-scaffolding 37, 54, 61–62; by teachers 12, 19, 28, 31, 81
practice 7, 8–9, 12
praise 109, 111
preparation for working with a pupil 57–59
preparedness 7, 9–10, 12
primary schools: class-based support 3; cover supervisors 4; DISS project 6; group work 88; intervention programmes 108–109; number of TAs in 1; part-time TAs in 2; social skills 104; Thinking Together project 101
problem-solving: group work 88, 95, 97–98; growth mindset 41; independent learning 85; prompting 111; resilience 22; self-scaffolding 37, 38, 39, 54, 61, 62
process success criteria 32, 47–52, 57–59; assessment for learning 78–79, 115, 118; giving feedback to teachers 80, 82; group work skills 98; self-assessment 85; self-scaffolding 62, 63; *see also* mini-goals
product success criteria 47–48
professional development 18, 72, 73, 111
professional identity 21
programme fidelity 106
progress: assessment for learning 78, 111; benchmarking 80; DISS project 6; giving feedback to pupils 83–84; intervention programmes 105, 107, 108; mini-goals 31, 37, 38, 48, 52; monitoring 21, 32, 62; scaffolding process 46; self-assessment 85; SEN Code of Practice 19; tracking and assessment 104
prompt sheets or cards 61, 62, 65–66
prompting 53, 54, 59, 63–66, 68, 89, 111; assessment for learning sheet 118; commentary on extract 116, 117; giving feedback to teachers 82; intervention programmes 109; peer support 90; self-evaluation 18; studying your interactions 71–73
puppets 93

questions: diagnostic 46–47, 57, 84; dialogic talk 35; exploratory talk 101; open 9, 35, 112; peer support 90–91, 93; questioning skills 35, 38; *see also* clueing; prompting

reading 4, 28, 103
recasting 69
record-keeping 76, 80–81, 107–108
repair role 20
reports, end-of-year 77
research 5–11, 111–112
resilience 11, 22
resources 57, 62, 104, 106
respect 95–96, 97, 102
responsibility: group work 95; pupils 32, 38, 46, 52, 57, 67, 110, 112; teachers 19, 109; *see also* independence
reviewing success at a task 54, 61, 62
roles of teaching assistants 2–5, 7, 12, 18, 19–21, 110
Ross, G. 32, 44

saying nothing 64, 112; *see also* silence
scaffolding 13, 17, 19–20, 32–33, 43–56, 57, 110; contingency 46–47; definitions of 43–44; formative assessment 78; framework for 21–23, 53–55, 59–60, 73–75, 92–93, 112; giving feedback to teachers 76; group work 94, 95; independent learning 85; intervention programmes 109; process of 45–46; process success criteria 47–52; pupil-to-pupil 88–93; self-assessment 85, 86; self-evaluation 18; *see also* self-scaffolding
schemas 25
scribing 11, 85
scripts 68–69
secondary schools: asking teachers for support 22; cover supervisors 4; DISS project 6; group work 88; intervention programmes 108; number of TAs in 1; part-time TAs in 2; social skills 104; subject specialists 3; Thinking Together project 101
self-assessment 79, 84–87
self-esteem 20, 23; *see also* confidence
self-evaluation 17–18, 111
self-help strategies 66
self-scaffolding 37–40, 46, 70, 110–111, 112; commentary on extract 116, 117; development of internal monologue 47; group work 88; growth mindset 41;

prompts 65, 89; scaffolding framework 53, 54, 59, 60–63, 93
SEN *see* special educational needs
SEN Code of Practice 19, 81, 86, 103, 104, 105, 108
SENCOs *see* special educational needs coordinators
sharing ideas 98
silence 64, 66, 72, 116
skills: CBI report 11; exploratory talk 101; fixed versus growth mindsets 40; group work 95–98, 99, 100, 102; intervention programmes 104; self-scaffolding 41; skills pupils bring to a task 31; social 89, 95–96, 103, 104; social constructivist learning theory 30; zone of proximal development 28
social constructivist learning theory 24, 25, 26–27, 30–31, 34
social skills 89, 95–96, 103, 104
special educational needs (SEN): diagnostic tests 77; DISS project 6, 7–8; effects of 'Velcro' model of support 7–8; intervention programmes 103, 104–105, 108; one-to-one support 3, 8; SEN Code of Practice 19, 81, 86, 103, 104, 105, 108; teacher's role 12
special educational needs coordinators (SENCOs) 13, 19, 74, 103, 105, 107
speech interventions 4
spelling 4, 33–34, 103
SPRinG project 94–98, 99, 101
stigmatisation 22
structured help 44–45, 57
subject knowledge 4, 9, 106–107
subject specialists 3, 107
summative assessment 77–78, 79; *see also* assessment
support, definition of 44
support role 20

talk: dialogic 34–37, 41; EDTA project 112; exploratory 94, 99–102; group talk rules 96, 97, 98; ineffective 111; IRF pattern 33–34, 35, 36
'talk partners' 98
tally chart 72–73
task completion 9, 112
teachers: administrative support for 4; dialogic talk 35; end-of-year reports 77; freeing up 23; giving feedback to 20, 47, 75, 76, 79–83, 95, 109, 111; group work

94, 95; intervention programmes 103,
104, 106, 107, 109; IRF pattern 36; lack
of preparedness 9; liaison time with 10,
12; making learning relevant 31; observing
71–72; partnership with TAs 13; planning
for changes to practice 114–115; process
success criteria 49, 50; pupils asking for
help from 22, 62; roles and responsibilities
12, 18, 19, 110; SEN pupils separated
from 8; zone of proximal development 28
technology 26–27
Thinking Together project 96, 101
tracking 104
training 9, 12, 20; ELSAs 5; subject
knowledge 4, 107; video recording
interactions 73
trust 95–96
'two stars and a wish' 86

'Velcro' model of TA support 7–8, 10
verbal commentary 45, 68–69, 86

verbal prompts 65; see also
prompting
video recordings 72, 73, 74, 101
vocabulary 63
Vygotsky, Lev 25, 26, 27, 99

waiting time 64, 66, 72, 116
Webster, Rob 8
welfare support 4–5
whole classes, leading 4
whole-school approach 75, 112
Wider Pedagogical Role (WPR) model 7, 8,
10, 12
Wiliam, Dylan 79, 83, 84
Wood, D. 32, 44
working hours 2, 10
writing 4, 103

zone of learning 31–32
zone of proximal development (ZPD) 27–28,
31, 41, 44, 63, 94, 96